Rescued
Out of the Shadows

Short stories of rescued dogs coming "out of the shadows" and into light and love

by
B. K. Stubblefield

Rescued - Out of the Shadows

Short stories of rescued dogs coming "out of the shadows" and into light and love

First Edition
Copyright © 2015 Birgit Stubblefield
ALL RIGHTS RESERVED

No part of this book may be reproduced in any form, by photocopying, or by an electronic or mechanical means including information storage or retrieval systems without written permission from the author/copyright holder.

NOTE: While the stories in this book were inspired by real events, some liberty has been taken in retelling the stories herein. Details have been added where they were lacking, and other authorial choices were made for the sake of the story or to protect the privacy of the individuals involved.

Photo Credits:

Jim Collings - Hannah Mae and Honey Bea

Rebecca Eaves – Frodo

Kimberly Marie – Ellie May

Walter Oster – Rosie & Liberty

Debbie Howe – Homer

Brandy Worland – Ottis

Marnie Claggett Photography – Abby

Cindy Thomas Photography – Barktown Rescue

Dedication

To my husband, Bob, who encouraged me to continue writing for no other reason than "just because".

Without his unwavering love and support the stories of these four legged friends and family members would not have come to light.

In letting me tell their stories I have encountered the worst and the best in humanity. I will always love you my dear husband, and all of our pets past and present.

Introduction

I am only one woman – a woman on a mission to make a difference.

As a little girl I always wanted a dog; just a small dog to love and cuddle and care for. Growing up in Germany in a small apartment with a younger sister and brother it was not an option for my parents to add a dog to the mix. I know that now but at the time I longed for a furry companion more than anything. My siblings and I were allowed to keep one small pet bird each – three little creatures to take care of – but it was no substitute for my desire to have my own dog. During every school break I looked forward to visit my Grandma and Grandpa and their dog Purzel.

Purzel was a grey wire haired dachshund with beautiful big brown eyes. He had a sweet and patient disposition towards a small girl who constantly fussed over him with a hairbrush and a comb. This is how my love affair with dogs began.

It would not be until many years later that I actually owned my first dog - a Shepherd/Collie Mix named Jessie. Others followed – small and large- and each one of them took their special place in our family. Without exception, all of them were loveable creatures and I dearly miss them still. At the end of December 2013 my husband Bob and I welcomed Harper to our home. Our two sons are adults and have long ago left the nest - and so it had become a bit quiet in our home since we said the final goodbye to our beloved St. Bernard/Collie Mix Sabo four years earlier.

Harper presented a challenge like none of our furry kids before him. Growing from a cute 10-week old little fur ball into a puppy that seemed to be on steroids, our patience was tested daily for what seemed to be an endless amount of time. His story and how we overcame some of the obstacles is told in "Rescued: A Tale of Two Dogs".

So many people fall in love with a cute little puppy without consideration to the size or the traits typical for a particular breed; especially difficult to predict when adopting a "mutt". Others think of these living, breathing creatures as fabulous Christmas gifts for the kids – so pretty to look at and so cute with a bright bow around the pup's neck.

Often the love and affection ends when the "gift" starts peeing and pooping all around the house or the little rascal finds everything worthy to be chewed on. Typically our four legged kids don't discriminate between the old house slippers and the new, long admired and terribly expensive designer shoes.

At the brink of finding another home for Harper, I spent every free minute of my day to find a solution to his impossible puppy behavior. Spending hours on the internet to search for training methods and other type of support, I also came across heartbreaking stories of incredible inhumane and brutal acts against man's best friend at the hands of their human owners. And so my mission begins.

This book was born to expose some of the unspeakably sad things these dogs had to endure, often right in our own backyards but hidden from sight and unknown to most of us. It also hails the unselfish actions of their rescuers and adoptive parents - many of them taking in "just one more" rescue because their heart can't tell them no. It has restored my faith in humanity.

Table of Contents

CHAPTER	PAGE
From Rags to Riches	13
Frodo	23
Ellie May	31
Rosie	39
Homer	51
Ottis	57
Abby – A Reverse Rescue	71
Barktown Rescue	77

Prologue

How many animal shelters, animal rescue groups, veterinarians, vet-techs, volunteers, animal advocates, volunteers, foster parents and pet adopters are working every single day with passion in their hearts and tears in their eyes to save an animal? An animal whose plight would otherwise be certain death! The answer is simple – too many!

Countless non-kill shelters and rescue organization across the nation are overwhelmed with the number of animals to take in and provide shelter, food, medicine, and give a whole lot of love to. These are the lucky ones; lucky because they have made it this far. And if luck continues, they will be housed, fed, bathed, fostered and medically cared for until they are adopted into their forever home.

While many of our fur friends at shelters or rescues are waiting for adoption day and to become a member of an accepting and loving new pack again -a.k.a human family- many of the circumstances that placed them into shelters could have been avoided.

Almost daily we hear and see the cries for help from animal rescuers to place the unwanted and discarded. And sometimes we hear about cases that go beyond unwanted and discarded and leaves us speechless with bleeding hearts. Cases of animals so severely neglected, misused and abused that only an army of dedicated trained professionals and trained volunteers can begin the healing process for this animal we call "Man's Best Friend".

Without this army of professionals and volunteers dedicated to provide a secure environment, medical treatment and rest, many precious lives would be lost without anyone ever hearing their cries for help. These professionals and volunteers are true heroes! They fight for the animals' lives often with their own funds and always with their own time to lift spirits, give hope, and with love they'll teach these broken souls to trust again. And they fight on the legal front - fighting for the animals' rights by working with the authorities to locate and prosecute the abusers. While having success, much work remains to be done. Sadly, in 2013 the State of Kentucky still ranked #50 in the "Worst Five" States category of the U.S. Animal

Protection Laws Ranking, published by the Animal Legal Defense Fund. Find out how your State ranks by visiting www.aldf.org.

One of these organizations that is dedicated to take care of and heal the most neglected and broken animals is "The Arrow Fund ", located in Louisville, KY who has generously allowed me a glimpse into their daily work and struggles to save as many animals as possible. Work that can take an emotional toll and leave one fatigued and feeling like drowning in a riptide of swirling dark waters.

Although not every animal can be saved because of injuries sustained beyond healing, the spirit of this dedicated and generous group of men and women has lifted many dogs out of deplorable situations. They brought them out of the shadows and into the light and placed them in the "right" home – a loving family.

Honey Bea and Honey Mae

From Rags to Riches

The Devil

The devil started his work in the wee hours of the morning. Just before dawn, under the cover of night, a shapeless vehicle driven by a faceless shadow illuminated only by the dashboard lights drives down a silent country road in rural Pike County, Kentucky. Purposely, but without hurry, the vehicle moves in the stillness of the early morning hours carrying the devil to his destination far enough from his lair so it cannot be found and identified later after his work is complete and the deed is done. Headlights are cutting through the darkness in search for just the right location.

Suddenly the vehicle slows and pulls over to stop on the side of the road, next to a gully now dry and covered with brush and weeds bordering farm land. The devil opens his door, steps out of his vehicle, silently and casually walks around the car where he then pulls open the passenger door. His hand reaches into the vehicle to pick up a bag lying on the passenger side floorboard. Whimpering noises are coming out of the bag but he pays no attention to the noise or the slight squirming. With one swift motion of his strong arm he picks up the bag and tosses it behind him into the tall weeds. The bag lands with a thud but the devil does not hear or see any of it as his faceless shadow moves back into his vehicle. The devil's work here is done.

*****

Becky and Jim

"Becky, are you going to the pet blessing and pet memorial at St. Andrews today?" Jim calls from the kitchen. "No, I am not going" Becky calls in reply. Becky is surrounded by fall decorations she pulled out of boxes earlier that day and is busy decorating the outside and inside of their beautiful home. It is a perfect, slightly crisp October day with a hint of fall in the air. It feels good after an early and unusually hot summer that seemed to last forever.

"Becky, are you sure you don't want to go?" Jim inquires again a little later. "I am SURE I'm not going" Becky replies a second time. Memories of Buddy Christopher, Becky's and Jim's beloved Beagle mix, is making Becky's heart heavy today. Buddy Christopher was adopted 9 years earlier and rescued from a life on the streets. Starved, underweight, with his pads damaged and other health issues, he chose Becky and Jim for his new family – and he got his way. It was a challenge to nurse Buddy Christopher back to health. Devoted to making Buddy whole again, Becky and Jim gave Buddy a loving home with all the comforts for a luxurious doggy life. Buddy Christopher's life ended two months earlier and Becky missed Buddy dreadfully.

Not easily persuaded, Jim calls Becky a third time "Are you sure you don't want to go?" Without hesitation "Oh well, yes I think I'll go" comes the reply this time. A couple weeks earlier Jim had registered Buddy to be included at the name reading of deceased pets at the St. Andrews Episcopal Church's pet memorial. Becky knows this will be the final goodbye and will help her and Jim to let go of Buddy Christopher. It was clear for Becky that after Buddy there would be no more dogs; she just could not bring herself to look at another. So the decision is made to attend the pet memorial together and unbeknownst to Becky or Jim a new journey of dog rescue has been set in motion and is about to begin.

*****

Line Man

It's going to be another scorching hot day in Pike County, Kentucky. Billy is already sweating as he begins his early morning work, hoping for a break from the unrelenting heat and dry conditions. The weather forecast does not promise relief any time soon. On this morning his work as a gas lineman takes him along a lonely stretch of country road in Pike County. Suddenly his eye catches a bag of dry dog food on the side of the road. *"Unbelievable how some people just don't care and leave their trash anywhere"* is his first thought. Moving to pick up the unsightly trash he suddenly registers movement from inside the bag. *"What in the world!?!....The bag is moving!!!"* is his second thought. What makes the bag move is the biggest surprise and makes this tough guy's stomach lurch. Expecting to find a small animal curiously checking out the dry dog food bag in search for a little food, Billy instead finds another garbage bag inside. Not knowing what to think or what to expect he carefully pulls out the garbage bag. Already baking in the morning sun the bag is hot and smells badly, emitting week cries. Carefully Billy opens the garbage bag, a foul odor wafting towards him. Billy does not register what he is looking at first. Quickly he realizes that what appear to be three tiny birds with four legs are actually three tiny puppies! Three tiny, living puppies, no bigger than birds, stuffed in a garbage bag, double wrapped and disguised in a bag of dry dog food, thrown away on a stretch of lonely country road to be baked to death by a hot summer's sun! Billy's stomach clenched as waves of nausea are rising like whipped up waves in a storming sea. This was the work of the devil and Billy lost his breakfast seeing it.

*****

Emergency

Another emergency phone call – this time from a shelter in Pike County – has Rebecca, Founder and Director of The Arrow Fund, responding in a hurry. Earlier this morning the shelter director received three puppies found on the side of a road by a line man. The puppies were barely hanging on to their lives. Hurriedly Rebecca grabs her car keys and makes a frantic dash to her car while filling in her husband Baxter on the phone call she just received. Together they are on their way to Pikesville. Racing against time, Rebecca ignores speed limits in hopes to win this race for life or death. The landscape flies by in a blur; saving these poor babies is all that matters. When Rebecca arrives at her destination, the three pups, two girls and a boy about four weeks young are in critical condition. They are barely alive. The little boy is in worst shape. He endured the brunt of the heat as his body was lying on top of his sisters. Although still alive at this time the little boy does not survive the ordeal. Suffocating, his body was the shield protecting the girls somewhat from the brutal summer sun, ultimately saving their lives. The following weeks are challenging for the pups and Rebecca alike.

The initial examination at the veterinary clinic reveals both puppies are afflicted with sarcoptic mange. Caused by sarcoptic mites, the skin disease can be life threatening and is contagious to humans. The parasite burrows deep under the skin, causing intense itching and with continuous scratching that will lead to hair loss. For the duration of treatment, the puppies will need to be quarantined. Without hesitation Rebecca transforms her bathroom into an ICU unit to care for the two surviving puppies, Hannah Mae and Honey Bea. Protecting herself by wearing gowns, special shoes and gloves she sets out to administer treatment in her home in coordination with the veterinary clinic. For the next four weeks, this is Rebecca's daily routine to treat the puppies. Providing 24 hour care, treating the contagious skin condition and hand feeding finally turn the fates of Hannah Mae and Honey Bea. As they grow, become stronger, and their skin condition improves, they turn into adorable honey colored puppies. The two "naked birds" turn into two beautiful, playful Terrier mix puppies who by now are inseparable. A tight bond between them is present and strong. Rebecca's work is almost done.

She has taught the "little birds" to fly; but now it is almost time for them to leave the nest.

*****

Rebecca Eaves arrives at St. Andrews Episcopal Church to ask for the blessings for her four legged foster children. Today Rebecca will be asking for a special blessing for two of her foster kids, Honey Bea and Hannah Mae. It is a busy scene with many people milling around with their pets in their arms or in carriers, and their dogs on leashes. As humans greet each other and shake hands, their dogs excitedly bark about all the activities and they greet and get to know each other in typical doggy fashion, sniffing each others' butts. An atmosphere mixed with hope, expectation, devotion, renewal and healing is in the air.

Rebecca is still getting situated when a woman approaches her, pointing to an igloo shaped cat carrier Rebecca is holding in her hand asking "Do you have kittens in there?" the woman inquires. "No, I have two little pups" answers Rebecca, adding "Would you like to see them?"

The woman standing in front of Rebecca is Becky Collings. "Sure I would like to see them" Becky replies and out came two tiny little creatures. Meanwhile Becky's husband Jim has made his way over to check out what Becky is fussing over. "Oh my God, what is that?!?" Jim exclaims. "These are two little pups! Have you ever seen anything so cute in your life?" Becky cries with a glow on her face and a sparkle in her eyes.

This is how Becky and Jim met Rebecca Eaves, Director and Founder of the Arrow Fund in Louisville, Kentucky. Not yet realizing it – they had also just met their new fur babies, Hannah Mae and Honey Bea!

*****

Adopting again?

After the ceremony at St. Andrews Episcopal Church is over and the Collings' are on their way home, a little seed has been planted in both of their hearts. Cuteness overload could not and would not be resisted!

At their short visit at the church Hannah Mae seems to have chosen Jim for her potential new Dad. "Can you believe how tiny they are, and how cute?" Jim asks Becky. "That little Hannah Mae really took to me. I think she wanted to come home with us" Jim keeps saying. "And Honey Bea…what a sweet little girl" Becky responds. Their minds and hearts could not comprehend the evil done to these innocent little creatures.

There was only one small hurdle. Under no circumstances would Rebecca allow for separate adoptions. They needed to stay together, no matter how long it would take to find a new home for them. Period. After sharing the struggles for survival together Hannah Mae and Honey Bea still depend on each other and continue to need each other. One is never found without the other. Short separations from each other cause severe anxiety.

But how could anyone choose which one to adopt? Actually, for the Collings' this was not a question. Once the decision was made to adopt it was easy to adopt both puppies. And so the application was filled out and a new chapter was about to begin for Hannah Mae and Honey Bea, and of course for Becky and Jim.

*****

If you ask Rebecca she will tell you that any prospective adopter will be scrutinized, taken under a microscope and strip searched. Well, maybe not strip searched but checked out in any legal way possible to ensure all adoptable animals will end up in caring and loving homes. It would be a devastating scenario for rescuers and animals alike if any animal found itself once again in a negligent or abusive situation.

Rebecca was not surprised to receive the adoption application for Hannah Mae and Honey Bea shortly after their chance meeting. Something had "clicked" and Rebecca had a "feeling". The usual approval procedures were applied and surprise…Rebecca finds out they share the same Veterinarian! A phone call to Dr. Richard Goranflo produces a glowing review for the Collings. He knows Becky and Jim through Buddy Christopher and Rebecca finds out quickly that an adoption by the Collings' would be a match made in heaven. Rebecca deeply respects Dr. Goranflo and his work. Helping The Arrow Fund with some of their initial cases, Rebecca witnessed his experience and caring with her animals and has come to know him well. This was great! It was the perfect reference and the perfect home for Hannah Mae and Honey Bea.

Everything is coming together! One has to be curious …was this a chance meeting or divine intervention?

*****

Adoption Day

Today is the day! All formalities have been met and the path for adopting Hannah Mae and Honey Bea has been cleared.

The day is filled with emotions. Thinking about Buddy Christopher, the challenges he faced early in his life, his quirks, but mostly the happy times Becky and Jim shared with him is crossing both of their minds. Buddy has cleared the path to open their hearts to love again. Two big personalities in two tiny packages are awaiting their new home.

An igloo shaped carrier sits on the back seat of Becky and Jim's car, similar to what the two puppies are accustomed to while recovering under Rebecca's care. This will be their new safe haven for the next few weeks until they are fully acclimated and at home with Becky and Jim.

The meeting and exchange takes place in Dr. Goranflo's office. Everyone is excited. Many people have had a hand in making this event possible. Caring people like Bill who paid attention to a thrown away dry dog food bag, the shelter director who knew about and called The Arrow Fund, Rebecca Eaves who selflessly spent hours to treat and attend to two puppies who were deemed to be minutes away from death's door, Blue Pearl Veterinary Clinic who oversaw the treatment and monitored the healing progress, St. Andrews Episcopal Church where the initial meeting took place, and of course Becky and Jim who selflessly opened their heart to two of the cutest little kids on four legs anyone can imagine.

*****

Author's Note

Hannah Mae and Honey Bea are two of the luckiest dogs. After their horrific ordeal they truly hit the jackpot. Still very much dependent on each other and never far apart, they have adapted well to their new home and surroundings. Hannah Mae adopted Jim and would not move from his side during my visit to their home. Honey Bea settled in with Becky and stayed on her without budging. They are two healthy and happy dogs, and how could they not be? Treated like doggie royalty they sleep in their own bedroom, on a bed fit for a queen with the ceiling fan running for comfort. They dine on the most delectable dog food, receive regular professional grooming and are ALWAYS surrounded by people who share their love freely.

The devil did not get his way. Divine intervention – for this was truly a match made in heaven!

Frodo

Frodo

Hi – My name is Frodo. I am a very happy dog and just love everyone. I only have three legs but that doesn't bother me none. I get around just fine and I don't even miss it! My human Mom loves me so much and I love her more. She buys food especially for me, and always has real yummy treats for me…but she hides them in a silly little toy. She does not understand that I can dig any treat out from anywhere!

Mom also buys me other toys to play with. I love toys; especially the ones with this white cottony stuff inside. I know a neat trick where I put a little hole in the toy and then pull all that fluffy stuff out. It looks like little snowballs. I do this every time my Mom buys me this kind of toy because I like making snow for her! I heard her say she likes fresh snow.

I have the best time when Mom takes me out on walks, and sometimes she allows me to go with her to visit Aunt Leslie. Aunt Leslie has a cool store with a rabbit in the back room. Now the rabbit is kind of boring so I really don't play with him. But I love to play with other dogs.

The last time we visited Aunt Leslie's store there were so many people there. They were all so friendly and everyone wanted to pet me and have their picture taken with me. It was really fun! They had food and other stuff and made a big deal about a lady who painted my picture. Everyone said I was a famous dog and should act that way, but…I would much rather sniff them and lick their hands and faces. I heard that some people from far away countries wrote to my Mom to ask about me and how I was doing.

I am doing fine. Life is great and full of fun. I am such a happy dog!

*****

Frodo's Journal - Code Red

"En route now- dog duct taped - mauled – en route to Blue Pearl. Prayers please – This is bad! Already know donations are needed".

So starts the journal on this 2nd day of July in 2013, another case of life and death for The Arrow Fund in Louisville, KY. By no means a "typical" case even for The Arrow Fund whose mission is to take cases of the most neglected and abused animals to provide immediate and lifesaving medical assistance. Not a typical day at all.

The call comes in from Metro Police. A dog is found in Louisville's West End, a section of the city where underground dog fighting is a common occurrence. Hidden well within a thriving city sophisticated underground, dog fighting operations provide a form of entertainment with thousands of dollars at stake; a barbaric blood sport with levels of sophistication for the purpose of competition, entertainment, status and of course wealth.

Two year old Frodo is found chained to a fence with a short, thick chain around his neck. He is partially covered by an old filthy mattress leaning against the fence to shield him from the view of possible bypassers. His small space is covered in feces and filth. Barely able to move, his back leg is broken in multiple places and has atrophied with new wounds from more recent attacks. He is badly hurt; his body is battered and covered with bite wounds on his torso, legs, scrotum and ears, too many bite wounds to count. His front leg is badly injured and already shows signs of infection. Later it is found that not only his leg but his bone is infected as well.

As if this is not enough to break the spirit of this badly injured dog, his muzzle is wrapped with duct tape and bite wounds from behind detach the top of his muzzle. Both canines are embedded in his mouth with bone fragments attached and infection setting in. Frodo is a bait dog. He is being used for fight dogs to practice on. His muzzle taped with duct tape ensures that he can't fight back, making him a helpless victim. He is being used until he dies. No one expects him to live and no one cares. There are always more dogs to be found, given away for free, stolen or lured away from their homes, and Frodo is easily replaced.

Perhaps he was meant to be a fight dog and was supposed to be trained to become a fierce killer but refused to fight and therefore failed? Maybe he was someone's pet stolen right out of his home? Or perhaps he was becoming too big or too much for his previous owner and was therefore advertised for "free" on Craig's List? No one will ever know where Frodo comes from. What is known at this very moment is that his life is hanging by a thread. One more round of baiting will definitely finish him off and will kill him. But…dogs like Frodo are expandable in this bloody sport.

"Frodo will need surgery to be able to eat again. This boy is in extreme pain upon arrival at Blue Pearl Animal Hospital. His broken and battered leg will need to be amputated but he is too weak now," reads the entry into The Arrow Fund's blog.

Rebecca is by Frodo's side, telling him "No one will ever hurt you again" while petting him gently. As if understanding that he is now safe, Frodo lights up as if to say "Someone is actually being nice to me"? Frodo is now under the care of The Arrow Fund and he is safe, but he will have much healing to do.

The first night in the safety of Blue Pearl Animal Hospital is fairly calm. Frodo is heavily medicated for pain while receiving fluids and antibiotics through an IV. Upon arrival and intake at the Blue Pearl Animal Hospital Frodo undergoes mouth surgery to re-attach his muzzle. Basically his muzzle is sewn back in place where it was ripped up from a bite wound and his uprooted teeth and still attached bone fragments are being removed. His puncture wounds are being cleaned and a drain is placed in his front leg. He also has an infection in his nose/sinus area.

Due to the conditions of his mouth and teeth, Frodo is starving. He has been starving for some time. Withdrawal of food is one method being used in the dog fighting training but with Frodo being used as bait, feeding him was not a concern of the trainers. The day after surgery Frodo is able to take in a little bit of food.

Already Frodo enjoys the company of the people around him. Rebecca blogs "When we are around him he really enjoys being petted. When I stop petting him, he scoots towards me begging for more. Bless his heart. Please send love and light to our boy".

Frodo has a lot of visitors today. Reporters from three news television stations are among his visitors who will tell his story and will ask for help in finding the men responsible for this unspeakable crime. Their reports will not only tell about Frodo's sad history and rescue, they will also bring attention to this illegal but widespread problem of dog fighting and associated crimes in our communities. Frodo's medical bills will be staggering; donations are needed... a lot of donations.

Two days after his surgery Frodo receives a break from IV's. He is being treated to a long visit from Rebecca and the best belly rub ever – most likely the first belly rub ever! He absolutely loves it! Rolling around on his back with his injured front leg sticking straight up in the air, his body stretched out, tongue lolling and big brown moist eyes dreamy; Frodo is a picture of happy contentment. But the happy picture is deceiving. Tomorrow he will face surgery to have his back left leg removed.

Four days after Frodo was found chained to a fence, starved, injured and in deplorable living conditions, he is taking his first walk outside. It is day one post-op and his surgery went well. His leg was removed up to his hip and he was neutered at the same time. Rebecca blogs "His recovery both physically and emotionally will be long-term. We are taking it one day at a time".

While many hands are busy to treat Frodo for his physical injuries, an army of volunteers is busy passing out over 500 flyers in the area where Frodo was found, seeking information leading to the arrest and conviction of the person or persons responsible. Frodo's plight has come to the attention of The Humane Society of the United States who offers a $5,000 reward for anyone coming forward with information leading to the arrest of the people involved in the cruel and abusive activity of this dog fighting ring. Volunteers are going from house to house in the neighborhood Frodo was found in, knocking on doors, talking to as many people as possible trying to find information and the persons responsible for this crime. "A clear message is being sent that this type of violence and crime is not accepted in our city," states Rebecca.

It is now day eight after surgery and Frodo is doing well. He is now in the care of All Pets Veterinary Center who will help him recover from his wounds. Thanks to Dr. Jewell, Frodo's Veterinarian and her expert medical care, he is making great strides towards recovery. The incision where his leg is amputated looks good and Frodo is on his way to recover physically and mentally. Dr. Jewell, along with all the staff at All Pets Veterinary Center, makes sure he receives a lot of loving as well. The entire staff at All Pets Veterinary Center can't get enough of petting and loving this special boy.

Just a couple of days later, day ten after his rescue, Frodo melts hearts when for the very first time he plays with a stuffed animal. This is no small feat as it is part of testing his reaction to new things presented to him. It is the beginning of being exposed to new activities and situations for the next days and weeks ahead. "We are taking it slow with this baby that has seen so much torture and cruelty," informs Rebecca to the many followers of her blog. "With the amount of cruelty and torture this baby has seen we want to set him up to succeed by introducing him very slowly to all situations that he will encounter. So far he is just wowing us with his amazing personality"!!!

Belly rubs have become a daily routine Frodo is looking forward to. As he thrives and becomes healthier, his physical and emotional wounds are beginning to heal. He loves visitors – he loves their non-threatening smell, their kind, soft words, and their kind hands that do not inflict pain but instead pet him gently and rub his belly. Courtney, a volunteer for The Arrow Fund, curls up with him and reads aloud from a book. Frodo is in heaven; he shows no signs of aggression. Instead he makes a great snuggle partner!

July 23rd – by now Frodo has been taken in by The Arrow Fund. He is a quick student who has learned to sit, stay and knows that every time he does something right he receives a treat. He loves his treats! Frodo is beginning to trust and slowly begins to forget the harsh treatment of the past. A sweet and goofy personality is emerging. Today he will have to undergo one more surgery to remove a tooth. This is nothing compared to the surgeries he has already had to endure upon delivery to the Animal Hospital after his rescue.

On August 13th Rebecca writes "Frodo is doing well. We are taking him out into the world and exposing him to all types of situations. We call them our "dates" – we go all over and of course he romps and plays and he always gets his kiddie cone ice cream treat. He loves them!"

During the next few days, Frodo will experience new excitements. His first play date with Louis – another Arrow Fund case – goes well. No aggression towards other dogs is detected, just romping, jumping, chasing and having fun. After a long play session he is exhausted. Gathering all his "babies" - numerous plush toys - around him Frodo takes a long, well deserved nap. With this simple act, he is stealing hearts.

By now he has become a sort of "celebrity". He is the poster boy for animal cruelty and has gathered attention from around the world. Rebecca blogs "Frodo will be going to Frankfort with The Arrow Fund on February 20 to Humane Lobby Day to help fight for stronger laws in our state. The laws to protect animals are THE WORST here in Kentucky! That is a fact!"

Frodo's story is heartwarming and full of hope. Considering the many cruel acts against him and the severity of his injuries he continues to amaze everyone with his goofy and happy personality. His wounds – physical and emotional - have healed. It was a difficult and painful road to recovery made possible only by dedicated people like Rebecca Eaves whose passion shines and her eyes mist when talking about Frodo and all her other cases she continues to take in. She states "This boy has never shown aggression after all he has been through… He is just one of the sweetest babies I personally have ever met. Those that have met him will agree".

Rescues like Frodo's would not be possible without skillful experts like Dr. Missy Jewell and an "army" of dedicated volunteers who tirelessly work to undo the wrongs inflicted by heartless and cruel individuals; individuals without conscience, and numb to the cries of pain of the animals trained to fight and ultimately rip each other apart. This is done in the name of the almighty dollar, for gang initiations, to boost ego and to gain status within a particular group. This has to be stopped! Tougher laws are needed to protect innocent animals and to punish those who continue to break existing laws. Everyone can contribute by being vigilant and being observant to any strange dog cries, unusual activities and foot traffic around abandoned homes. A larger number of pit-bull type dogs chained up in backyards can be a sign of dog fighting activities and should be reported to the authorities immediately. Sadly, often individuals are afraid to come forward and their silence is covered with a dark cloak of fear - fear of retaliation from the accused.

Unfortunately Rebecca's cry for help is echoed by too many organizations across the country. To fight neglect and abuse in all its ugly forms they will need our help.

"We have been hit hard with so many cases of severe torture, abuse, and neglect. Thank you all for your support – together we can make a difference. He (Frodo) is a big kisser and a perfect example for us not to give up on these creatures … we must all fight for them … we are their voice."

Thanks – Rebecca – The Arrow Fund

Authors Note

To find more information about what happens in a dogfight and how dog fighting is affecting people visit:

www.humanesociety.org/dogfighting.

The Humane Society of the United States will pay up to $5,000 for information leading to the arrest and conviction of a dogfighter.

Ellie May

Ellie May

The woman arrives at the address she was given earlier when the phone call came. Cautiously she is stepping out of her car as she surveys the area with all her senses on high alert. All is quiet; no noise is disturbing the early afternoon. No other car is in the driveway and no nosy neighbors are outside to observe or question her business.

Despite a rather chilly afternoon and a slight breeze brushing against her face with only a light jacket to provide protection, she is starting to sweat as an uneasy feeling is creeping up her spine. She is a brave and fearless woman but she knows to trusts her instincts for what she knows she will find.

Slowly but steadily she is advancing towards a large tool shed in the backyard. The woman knows she is trespassing but she is on a mission and won't be stopped. She can't see yet what she is looking for but the stench of decomposition is drawing her towards a kennel hidden behind the shed. She fears the worst.

Earlier that day Kimberly Marie received a phone call from the Weimaraner Rescue Organization where she volunteers asking her to check on a possible severe dog abuse situation. A neighbor in this suburban neighborhood called the organization reporting regular beatings, neglect and starvation of the animal. They have been listening to her cries and witnessed the beatings firsthand and they could no longer hold their silence. For a couple of days now the dog was lying seemingly motionless in her pen.

As Kimberly is reaching the pen the stench intensifies. At first glance the motionless animal appears to be dead but upon entering the enclosure and kneeling beside the dog, Kimberly notices the dog's eyes are opening and focusing on hers pleading for help.

Lying otherwise motionless and covered with filth and feces, the dog's left hind leg is badly injured. Flesh black and literally rotting off her leg is exposing bone. What happened to this once beautiful Weimaraner dog that caused an injury this severe?

What happened to this Weimaraner that her once beautiful grey coat is now covered in dirt and her graceful features are twisted in an expression of pain? There is nothing aristocratic about this dog's features or her filthy surroundings. She has been beaten and degraded to a lump of rotting flesh with her spirit broken.

*"Often referred to as the "grey ghost" because of the distinctive color of its short, sleek coat, the Weimaraner is a graceful dog with aristocratic features."

*"Lauded for his ability to work with great speed, fearlessness and endurance when on the hunt, the Weimaraner is also known for being an easily trainable, friendly and obedient member of the family. This is a breed that loves children and enjoys being part of his family's "pack."

Once upon a time this dog loved a child. She loved the child that is living at the house with the dog's abuser. In the beginning the child loved the dog and named her Ellie May. Gradually the visits from the child became fewer and fewer until the child no longer came to visit, pet, play or had a kind word for her. There were no more playtimes outside the pen; the kennel had effectively become Ellie May's prison. Ellie May was left and ignored with no chance of being part of her human "pack".

As much as she tried, Ellie May could not please her Master. Whenever he came to the pen she was happy seeing him, jumping and greeting him excitedly. This did not please the Master. At first he would smack her and yell at her to get away from him. With every visit to the pen he seemed to be more and more agitated at the dog's attempts to gain his friendship and love.

The Master's aggression towards Ellie May would increase with every visit. He would find reasons to slam his fist into her head, with his rising temper spurning him on to hit harder and harder, and battering her body with his iron fists. His screaming at the dog would tune out Ellie May's cries. She did not understand what she did to anger the Master so much. She is confused and fears every visit from him. She tries to be very still and invisible but it does not help. The Master is now angered by her pitiful sight. For no apparent reason things went out of control during one of the last visits from him. While pushing and kicking her, Ellie May loses her balance causing her hind leg to get caught up in a damaged section of the pen. The wire slices her leg deeply, leaving a large bleeding gash. The Master did not soften at the sight of the hurt animal but walked out of the pen without a second look. The Master did not care.

Gradually the time between visits would become longer and longer. Often the Master would forget to bring food for Ellie May. Occasionally a neighbor witnessing the continued abuse would feel sorry for the mistreated dog and sneak a treat to Ellie May when her Master was away.

On this particular day this neighbor made the call that would end Ellie May's until now miserable life with her cruel abuser. On this day the neighbor went again to see Ellie May and found her unresponsive in her pen, lying in the same spot she was laying in the day before. Apparently Ellie May had not moved in a couple of days. Weak from starvation, beatings and now an infection setting into her wound and spreading, she no longer had the strength to move. Fearing the dog might be dead, the neighbor found the courage to call the Weimaraner Rescue to report Ellie May and her location.

As Kimberly Marie knelt next to Ellie May caressing and assuring her that she would be taken care of, a man was fast approaching the pen yelling and shouting all the way. Where did he come from so suddenly? Perhaps he had been watching Kimberly's approach from the inside of his home? The man is Ellie May's Master and he is not happy about this strange woman having trespassed onto his property and now being inside the pen with Elli May. After all, this was his dog and he was about ready to deal with this sorry and injured animal his way. The plan was to just shoot her later because she was no good to him and he could not afford the vet bill anyway. Better to get rid of her now.

Little did the man know that this petite woman standing in front of him was not one bit intimidated by his rude and irrational behavior! Although her heart was racing by the unavoidable confrontation she was engaged in, she showed no signs of distress or weakness. Petite in stature she would not be a physical match to this irritated dog beater but Kimberly Marie was prepared should it come to a physical assault. Hidden by her light jacket was a Ruger 380 gun and she would not be afraid to use it. Long ago Kimberly Marie had obtained her license to carry a gun. This gives her the assurance and if necessary the protection to do what she needs to do in her line of rescue work. Standing her ground firmly she told the Master that she would take the dog to her veterinarian for treatment. A verbal argument was about to erupt when Kimberly changed her tactics and pleaded with the man to let her take the dog to her vet at no cost to him. She tried to convince him that Ellie May could be saved. Grudgingly the man finally gave in and told Kimberly Marie to just take the dog away and don't come back.

As Kimberly Marie is lifting the dog gently into her arms to carry her to the car, she is aware that the dog might try to bite as a way to protect herself from the pain she surely was in. To her surprise Ellie May lays her head on Kimberly's shoulder as if in relief; as if she knew that this gentle woman would save her life and rescue her from her miserable existence. As tears are welling in Kimberly's eyes, a heartstring is touched.

Upon arrival at the veterinary clinic it was determined that Ellie May's leg would need to be amputated up to her hip. Surgery took place immediately and went well. With expert veterinary care she started to heal. Her new place was on a soft dog bed instead a filthy dirt floor. Her bed was placed close to the reception area where she was surrounded by people treating her with love and care.

Every evening after work Kimberly Marie would visit Ellie May at the clinic, witnessing her progress firsthand. At first Ellie May would only be able to lift her head in greeting. As days went by and she regained some of her strength she would get up and greet Kimberly Marie happily as soon as she came through the door at her daily visit. Kimberly was convinced Ellie May did smile at her each time she saw her coming! It was amazing to watch Ellie May's progress and how quickly she was able to function so perfectly well on three legs.

Soon it was time for Ellie May to be released from her veterinary care. But now she needed a place to call home. Once again Kimberly Marie offered her assistance and promised to pick Ellie May up and transport her to a foster home or local rescue organization. But fate had other plans. Not quite ready to let her go Kimberly Marie spontaneously decided to foster Ellie May herself, provided that her other five dogs already calling Kimberly's place "home" would have no objections. Well, neither of the fabulous five objected and so Ellie May was adopted into the pack.

At first Ellie May had trouble walking on the hardwood floors in her new temporary home. True to her caring self Kimberly Marie laid rugs and towels around the house to help the dog get around. And moving around the house is what Ellie May did. As a matter of fact she did not leave Kimberly's sight and followed her every step. Without much notice Ellie May pulls a little more on Kimberly's heartstrings every day.

A few weeks have gone by and everyday life has settled into a routine. Six happy dogs greet Kimberly Marie every day after work with Ellie May always getting an extra pat and kiss on her head. After dinner, all the animals have equal cuddle time on the couch.

By now the time has come to seriously think about getting Ellie May adopted into a permanent home. The annual Weim and Cheese fundraiser and silent auction was coming up; an opportunity to meet and greet potential adopters. Usually this popular event would result in several dogs finding their forever homes; a happy ending for dogs and rescuers alike.

Kimberly Marie and Ellie May were making rounds greeting and visiting with potential adopters when a gentleman approached Kimberly with an adoption application in hand. Not prepared for what she would be asked Kimberly smilingly asks the adopter what dog he might be interested in. When she heard him answering that he was interested in Ellie May, Kimberly's heart dropped, her head started spinning and her eyes filled with tears. How could this be? No one wants to adopt a 3-legged dog! Why Ellie May…? Why…? Never thinking Ellie May would leave her but still to her own surprise she heard herself answering "I am sorry but she is not available, she is mine". And so Ellie May was "officially" adopted!

The bond binding them together was formed from the moment Kimberly May first saw Ellie May, a suffering creature lying motionless in her cage. In the end it could not be broken.

Kimberly's five dogs have adjusted well and also adopted Ellie May. She is now truly a member of a pack. Her once filthy fur has been restored to the shiny, sleek coat of the aristocratic "grey ghost".

Ellie May has taken her spot in Kimberly Marie's heart… and on her couch. Gone are the days of no human affection. There is no shortage of love and affection now. The hardwood floor is no longer an obstacle. Ellie May loves to play outside with her toys and she loves to chase the fabulous five. Ellie May is happy, healthy and whole again.

No charges were filed against the abuser by any of the parties. The risk of the abuser walking away with "a slap on his hand" under Kentucky's laws and having Ellie May returned to him as the rightful owner was just too great and was not a chance anyone wanted to take.

*****

*www.akc.org/breeds/weimaraner

I went out to rescue a dog that day
To give her a really good life
To take her away from the life that she led
And free her from trouble and strife

I thought I would do her a favor
And be a good person to her
And go do my bit for the country
I didn't go out on a spur.

But what do you think really did happen?
The day that I did my good deed,
I discovered a love that I'd dreamed of
And fulfilled in myself a strong need.

I now have a dog that I care for
I see things that I needed to see,
That lovely dog that I rescued
Really ended up rescuing me.

—By Kimberly Marie

Rosie

Rosie

Veterans Day 2014

The route in downtown Louisville is blocked off to traffic. It's a short route, just a few blocks, with both sides of the street lined by students from different schools each holding and waving an American flag, pride reflecting in their bright young faces. It sure is a sight to see stirring up different emotions for different people. It is a moment to honor, reflect and pay tribute to the ones who protect us and our freedom day in and day out and to those who came before them.

As Veterans Day Parades across the country are being held, over seventy units have come to march in the Louisville Parade. Veterans in full uniform, individuals and even three Medal of Honor recipients have travelled to be part of the celebration. There are displays of classic military vehicles, marching bands, parades of Veterans from years past all cheered on and saluted by sideline visitors.

Loud cheers erupt along the route as Walter Oster slowly drives his Hummer along the route, with his wife Janice marching alongside with a special charge by her side. Dressed in her Wounded Warrior vest Rosie walks every steps of the route with one missing leg. This is the second year for Rosie to walk in the parade and she has become quite the celebrity in Louisville's Veterans community. As the day unfolds, Walter smiles happily at Janice and Rosie, grateful to be an active participant as circumstances almost changed the events of this day. He smiles happily watching Rosie limping all the way to the finish line.

Who are Walter Oster and Rosie and why are they special?

*****

Walter

Walter's resume is an impressive one. Although officially retired now, protection was his business then and protection is his business still today. Drafted in 1966 during the Vietnam War he served and retired from the US Army, Military Police Intelligence Division followed by a twenty-six year career at the Louisville Police Department. Seventeen of those years he served in Criminal and Vice Intelligence Units as Detective.

Walter's continuous service and commitment to protection is evident is his many affiliations in Military Veteran's Affiliations – DAV Life Member (Disabled American Veterans), Member of USA Former Intelligence Ops and Life Member of the National Order of Trench Rats, *a secret, fraternal honor organization limiting its membership by selection only to those who show their devotion and meritorious service to the DAV and the welfare of the disabled veterans, his widow and orphans."

Not ready to settle into retirement upon taking his leave from the Louisville Police Department, Walter continues to work as an Investigator for the State of Kentucky for the next ten years. During this time he becomes aware of another type of crime that is common but so very often ignored; the crime against animals. To identify animal cruelty and bring the abusers to justice is fast becoming the focus of his attention. Clearly Walter sees the signs of dog fighting activities, caged and starving animals, and the horrible conditions of puppy mill breeding.

This is unacceptable for Walter and he is going to do something about it!

But this strong man who keeps in shape by training in his own gym and counts Hulk Hogan among his friends has a soft side well hidden within himself. Softened by the cries and haunted eyes of abused animals, Walter has dedicated his retirement to help this group of helpless victims. His hunting instincts are awakened and his senses sharpened once more. Walter knows how to bait and catch a criminal and he is watching. Walter is going to do something about it.

As a result of the some of these things going on in Louisville's West End he receives a call from a woman belonging to a group of people representing various "no kill" animal organizations. "Somebody gave us your name saying you are a retired police office. We want to feed the feral dogs and cats down there but are a little afraid without protection. Would you help us"? "Of course I would" Walters replies. He does not say no, or that he has no time. He offers his help readily and without hesitation.

As the group canvasses the area and tries to catch feral cats and dogs they are entering a building where to their horror they find a dog hanging from his neck…HANGING from his neck, still alive!!! Hanging from the ceiling is a white pit bull whose tail is wagging as people cautiously advance to rescue him from certain death.

*****

Using his skills acquired in over thirty years of intelligence and detective work, Walter applies those skills to track down the worst offenders. Long ago established connections serve him well. His name is passed within the crime fighting community. In working together with law enforcement agencies he tracks, reports and helps bringing convicted animal abusers to justice. Walter knows from experience that animal cruelty and interpersonal violence is linked as described in a recent letter from PETA to the 12th Circuit Commonwealth's Attorney Courtney T. Baxter regarding the animal cruelty case of a recently convicted dog killer.

This particular case is tragic in many ways. The torture inflicted is too graphic to describe and the author only wants to share that because of the actions of this young man, two of five dogs did not survive the ordeal, one escaped but could not be found, but luckily two dogs were recovered and nursed back to health. The offender is currently serving time in prison for his actions. What psychological barrier has been torn down to allow this type of cruelty to take place?

The other victim in this crime is the girlfriend who found the courage to file a police report about the torture and abuse. How was she was able to videotape the abuse of her puppies while it happened? What must she have been feeling to watch these horrible acts? Did she scream and beg to show mercy for her dogs? Did she yell at him to stop? Did her heart bleed? Threatening to kill her too if she would speak up, the abuser tried to intimidate her as a witness. Imagine her courage and strength to videotape and ultimately report the abuse of this killer!

In a letter to Attorney Courtney Baxter PETA requests "Because repeat crimes are the rule rather than the exception among animal abusers and given the malicious and violent nature of this case, we ask that, if convicted, the defendant be prohibited from owning animals for as long as possible."

Sadly this was not the first time for the young man had to answer to animal abuse charges.

In taking up the cause for our four legged friends Walter has seen many cases of abuse that won't let the fire in his belly burn out. Driven, he works on many cases assisted by his wife Janice, a board member for Crime Stoppers, and a circle of trusted friends.

*www.trenchrats.org

Rosie

"Who shot my dear Rosie"... is a burning question for Walter. It has become a very personal quest for Walter to find answers and get justice for Rosie.

March 13, 2013 is a mild and sunny afternoon in the West End of Louisville. After an especially long, cold and snowy winter season everyone is breathing a sigh of relief when finally a promise of spring is in the air.

Two teenage girls are happy to spend time outside doing what teenage girls like to do. Sitting side by side on the front steps of the porch they chat, giggle and banter with each other, enjoying the afternoon sun warming their young faces. A little black and white terrier mix belonging to one of the girls also enjoys her time with the girls outside. Sniffing and scratching the dirt she stays close and never wanders off too far. She is a good little dog and the girls don't pay too much attention trusting her to stay close.

Seemingly out of nowhere a black SUV suddenly stops in front of the house, and a young black male jumps out at the passenger side of the car with a 9 MM pistol in his hand. As the shot rings out the little black and white Terrier Mix, weighing no more than 20 pounds, is hit and crumples to the ground. The dog is screaming in agony and pain while at the same time the girls scream in fear and shock. The little dog is badly injured and needs help fast.

Curious neighbors from all around are rushing out of their homes to find out what just happened. Their faces are marked with anger, disbelief and tears when they see the small, badly injured dog. Emotions are running deep over this evil crime committed against this innocent creature.

Why did this happen? This incident happened so fast that the sequence of events is blurred in the minds of the girls - the witnesses to this crime.

In this section of town notorious for criminal activities the answer to this question is hard to find. Was it a gang initiation, an act of revenge or an afternoon entertainment for someone with no regard for life?

Police and Animal Control are called and both arrive quickly at the scene of the crime… possession of the animal is relinquished from the owner of the dog to animal control. Quickly the decision to euthanize this seriously injured young dog is made.

*****

But not so fast!

Word of the incident has reached Walter - he has no intention of letting this dog be euthanized without giving her a real chance for recovery. Arrangements with the Arrow Fund are made to deliver this poor dog to a Veterinary Clinic and try to save her life while official investigations into this crime have begun.

The little dog was named Rosie.

Frightened, afraid and shaky Rosie arrives at the Veterinary Clinic. After examining her injuries it is advised to amputate her front right leg up to her shoulder. The elbow area is shattered with bullet fragments throughout. A fragment has entered her chest but luckily did not enter her lungs. Rosie receives IV pain medication and fluids to comfort and ease her pain.

With no hesitation Walter agrees to assist with payments of the medical bills…

Was this the beginning of a new love affair for Walter?

Surgery to remove Rosie's right front leg went well. The little girl is tough and is coming through surgery just fine. She continues to be on IV meds and antibiotics and is monitored closely throughout the night.

"My wife Janice and I went to see Rosie a couple of days after her surgery at Blue Pearl Animal Hospital. I was melting because she was so sweet and I was also so furious over a driveby shooting of this innocent young dog" Walter recalls this first visit with Rosie with misting eyes.

In the afternoon of the second day after surgery the IV is removed and she receives medication in pill form. The very next day she will be released to her medical foster home where Rosie will be in expert hands to receive the medical care she needs.

Four days later something is wrong and Rosie is being rushed back to the Animal Hospital. Despite the expert care she is receiving from her foster mom, Rosie stopped eating and started shaking badly. It was determined that Rosie was actually in pain and needed her pain medication adjusted. Immediately Rosie starts eating again and the process of healing continues.

In the meantime the official investigations are aided by the community group "Kentucky Crime Stoppers".

Walters's wife and partner in fighting animal cruelty is a board member of the local Crime Stopper organization. Kentucky Crime Stopper is adopting Rosie's case and places a reward of $500 for information on this incident. This reward is offered in addition to Metro Police's reward of additional $500.

Walter organizes a group of volunteers to create, print and distribute flyers asking for information that would lead to the arrest of the shooter. The award amount jumps right off the flyer to grab attention. A group of passionate animal lover volunteers lead by Walter invade the streets surrounding the home of the incident. Protected by Walter and his concealed weapon, they are not afraid to knock on about five hundred doors. They talk to everyone available to obtain information about the identity of the shooter. "You must be either crazy, be a police man or carry a weapon" Walter is greeted in one instance. "You got two out of three right!" he easily replies.

To this date no one has come forward to claim the reward and bring the offender to justice.

"Whoever callously shoots a small dog in a driveby shooting will not hesitate to shoot a human being either. Thugs like this do not regard any life". Walter explains that the line between animal cruelty and crimes against humans is a small line too easily to be crossed. Not only was a small dog shot but an entire neighborhood was placed in danger.

Little Rosie is adjusting well thanks to a couple of "Angels" a.k.a medical fosters. Without these special fosters with their medical knowledge and their commitment to assist in the healing of the most severely abused animals, Rosie and many like her would not have the same chance of healing and ultimately survival.

About five weeks after Rosie was injured in this horrible crime, she is ready to be released from her foster care to go to her forever home. A tough guy with a big heart and a soft core who fell in love with her at the scene of her crime, along with his Crime Stopper wife, is ready to pick her up and take her to their home. Big smiles light up

Walter's and Janice's faces as they greet their new little girl. Cradling her carefully in his arms, Walter can't stop grinning. This girl belongs to him and he assures Rosie she is safe from harm now.

Just a little over one year later Rosie walks in her first Parade in the small town of Liberty, Kentucky. Together with Janice she walks the entire Parade from beginning to finish on her three legs beside an Army Hummer slowly driven by Walter. She is a strong little girl, made stronger by her loving human family.

It was a good day for Walter and Janice, spent with friends and their sweet dog Rosie. However, on this Fourth of July Holiday fate had plans for Walter and Janice to rescue another fur kid and for Rosie to get a playmate.

The phone rings and when Walter answers, she is talking to a woman who received his number from a friend. That is usually how it goes. His name is passed on in the rescue community whenever a case of animal cruelty is discovered.

The woman is telling him about two small dogs who were kept in a cage for three months, never seeing the light of day and today was the day they were going to be euthanized! The woman on the phone is begging for help. One of the girls was lucky to be placed with a family but the other was going to die today. "I'll take her" Walter responds without hesitating for even one second.

On the way back home to Louisville there is a new family member riding in the car with Walter, Janice and Rosie. Her name is Liberty! She is about nine months old, a brown "mutt" with big ears. Her little stump of a tail is wagging excitedly and big brown eyes are looking into a bright future, barely having escaped the talons of death.

Rosie is sharing her home with Liberty now and with Walter and Janice as their protectors. Although once severely injured, time has healed the physical and emotional scars.

According to Walter, Rosie's story unfortunately is not unique. Driveby shootings killing or severely injuring a dog is not uncommon in this particular section of Louisville. Today Rosie is adored by Walter and Janice beyond words. Her picture graces posters, t-shirts and sweatshirts to help raise awareness and to "STOP ANIMAL CRUELTY".

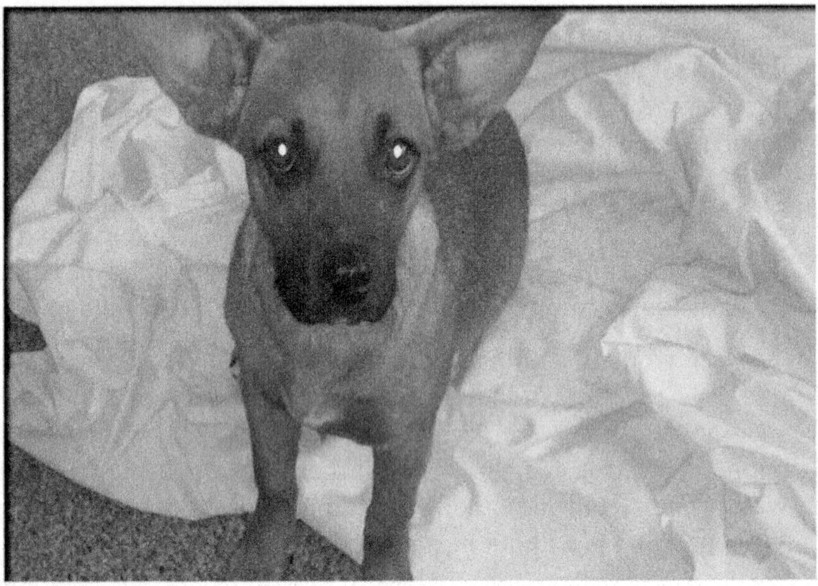

Liberty

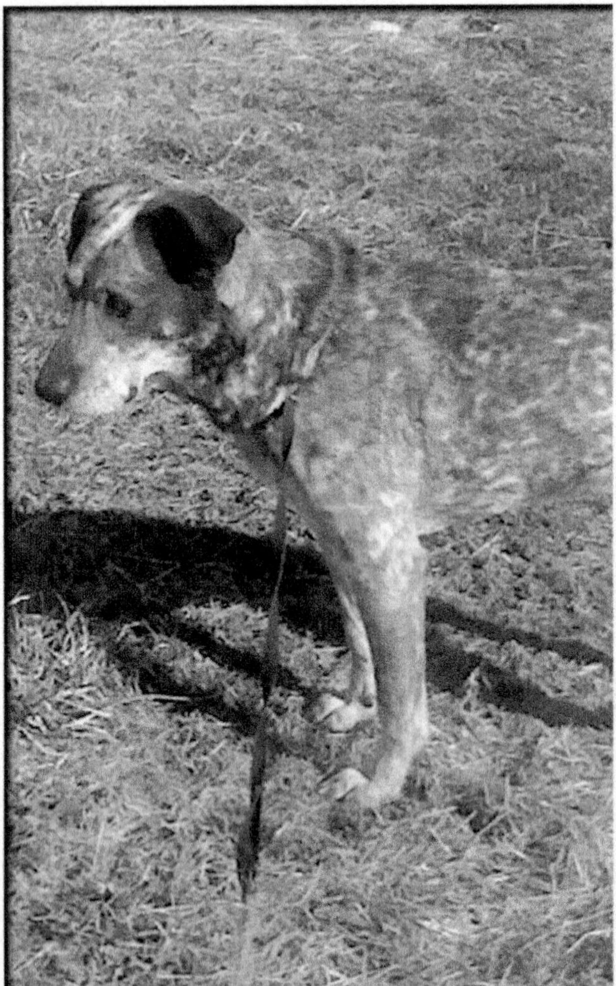

Homer

Homer

"It's official…..I have lost my mind at work today! Watching this little field mouse lying in the rain, I could not leave him there certain to drown in a puddle of water. I took him inside to dry him up. He is now chilling in a box at my house. I will take him back on Sunday to return him to his family. I AM NUTS"!

Debbie Howe's life is defined by different species of animals at home and at work. Every day when she shows up at work she is surrounded by up to thirty-five dogs of all sizes. Her job is best described as being the alpha dog or "pack leader" at a sophisticated doggie day care and pet provision center. Debbie has been observing and working with dogs all her life. Many years spent as Veterinary Technician and Dog Trainer have given her valuable insights of dog behavior. As a self-proclaimed loner she is often more comfortable around animals than people. "God gave me the love of animals and they have saved me through many bad things when I was a kid – they have saved me through many dark nights"!

It is apparent that Debbie has developed a way to communicate with animals in a way they understand, respect and therefore allow her to be their leader.

Each day at work Debbie greets every single dog with great affection and love upon their arrival. When her day at work is done and she arrives at her home, it is her turn to be greeted with great love and affection. Four furry rescue kids, a Rottweiler, a Pitbull and two Chihuahua/Yorkie mixes, all of them adopted from the county shelter and saved from death row just in time, are greeting her excitedly and with sloppy kisses. Her foster kids, two beagle mixes with stocky bodies and ears so large that they resemble more jackals than beagles, are also lining up for the daily meet and greet. Five rescue cats and two guinea pigs claim their share of space to complete this animal menagerie. No matter if Debbie is at work or at home, her charges are all "her kids".

One could argue that Debbie Howe indeed is "nuts" or that she simply is devoted to save, guard and protect every living creature, no matter how big or small. It's something Debbie has to do. She can't help it, it's in her blood.

Lucky for Homer!

Homer is the latest addition in Debbie's rescue collection of the unfortunate and unwanted motley crew. His name could not fit him any better in the saddest kind of way. Search results for the meaning of the name Homer show that it is of Greek origin and means "hostage"!

You see, his entire life Homer has been held hostage. He was put in a cage with no shelter at the age of eight weeks and never got out again. A life lived in a cage barely big enough to accommodate a growing puppy, Homer never experienced the touch of human affection and love. He never had a toy to play with to occupy his time or a gentle brushing to clean his dirty coat. At the age of 8 weeks Homer was put into a kennel – roughly 4 x4 feet – where he would remain for nine long years in solitary confinement until the day of his rescue during a brutally cold Kentucky winter in 2014. His owner did not care enough to clean his kennel and never freed Homer long enough to exercise his long legs as an adult dog. This spotted grey, red and black Red Heeler mix had grown into a large dog, his beauty hidden beneath a dirty coat with eyes filled with sadness and loneliness. Homer's bed was the hard packed dirt floor of his kennel where he not only slept but ate and relieved himself without much care from his owner. "Dog poop was piling sky high" says Debbie. This kennel was his prison and there was no escape. Often he would be hungry and thirsty while his food and water bowls remained empty. Homer was starving, his skinny body showing protruding ribs.

On January 7, 2014 an unusually cold and freezing winter day in Kentucky, the temperatures were zero degrees with wind chills much below zero. Animal Control was alerted to Homer's living conditions with a request to check into his welfare. With no shelter for warmth, no food and water frozen in his bowl, the day for Homer to be freed from his filthy prison had finally arrived. His owner willingly relinquished control because after all it was "too cold" to go out and feed him. A sloppy human in dirty clothing and living in filthy conditions himself did not have any sympathy for his freezing and starving dog. And so Homer's life was saved but his travels to happiness would first start with a stop at the County Shelter.

When a shaking, scared, malnourished and arthritis-ridden Homer arrived at the shelter, one can imagine the disappointment he must have felt when he found himself in yet another cage. For the first time in his life he received a bath, medicine to help ease the arthritis pain in his joints, a bed to sleep on and enough food to keep his stomach full. Every day the staff along with a number of volunteers visited Homer, socializing him, treating and speaking kindly to him, but... Homer was lonely.

After being at the shelter for six months Homer was sad and depressed. He began to become grouchy and started to bite. Although he had a bed to comfort his aching joints, Homer chose to sleep on the hard concrete floor. Blankets put on the hard floor by volunteers helped ease the bodily ache a little. Despite volunteers spending time with Homer the shelter environment put him in yet another stressful situation. He would barely eat; every bone in his body was showing. He needed to find a home!

The only problem was Homer was an old dog and it would be difficult, almost impossible, to place him with a family who would be able to fulfill his needs. Every attempt was made to find a home for Homer. An ad with his picture was listed in the weekly adoption section of the local newspaper and video clips were posted on social media, all to no avail... Homer was overlooked!

With every passing day his name inched up a little more on the list of death row inmates. Soon it would be his turn to leave his cell forever and take a walk through the door leading into doggy heaven. The hearts of the shelter volunteers were heavy. They were desperate to prevent the final walk and help Homer find happiness for his remaining natural years and made one last attempt that would change Homer's life and lead to a happy ending.

Enter Debbie Howe. A longtime friend of the Animal Shelter and certifiable "nuts" about rescue, she received a call from the Animal Control Director "I have an old one here, why don't you come and take a look at him and see if you can foster him" he asked Debbie.

"He got to me through his eyes" Debbie says. When she first saw Homer she fell in love with his eyes. In the space of a heartbeat a big, soulful and slightly bug-eyed look spoke volumes of pain, disappointments, heartbreak but also spoke of hope and a promise of forgiveness if only he could find someone to love him. His eyes touched Debbie's heart and awoke her instinct to protect another living creature once more. With mismatched eye colors – one eye golden brown, the other eye light blue, it was an interesting combination and a fascinating face to look at. "How could I leave this old and hurting hound behind?" Debbie asks herself.

Well, one look at this hound with his golden and blue eyes and their fate was sealed. They were kindred spirits. Arrangements were made to take Homer home. Debbie remembers this day well. "Climbing into the back seat of a friend's car with his arthritic hips turned out to be a bit of a challenge for Homer but he finally made it. He stuck his large head between the front seats and gave me a big sloppy kiss" she recalls.

Homer was on the road again, this time to a real home for the first time in nine years.

Today Homer claims roughly half a barn as his new home. The other half of the barn is taken up by small equipment and a goat pen. After nine years of solitude and no interaction and socialization his demeanor is guarded around Debbie's other dogs. He doesn't mind the goats too much and tolerates them when they are in their pen. He is a loner but he is happy. He feels secure in his dog cave but feels threatened when Debbie's dogs come too close.

His room contains an old mattress, hollowed out to accommodate a doggy heating pad. His dog bed rests on top of the mattress. This is where Homer sleeps now and where he hides his treasures.

Homer loves his "treasures" a.k.a toys. His prized possession is a squealing rubber pig. "When I come to the barn I can hear squeak, squeak, squeak...this is what he does when he hears me come," Debbie says.

When Debbie brings one of her dogs along Homer turns into a little hoarder. He hurriedly collects all his toys and takes them to his bed where he keeps close watch. They are "his" toys and "his" alone.

Homer's health has improved since he arrived at Debbie's home. His weight has changed from about 50 pounds to a healthy 80 pounds and his protruding ribs have finally disappeared. Thanks to daily doses of Glucosamine his arthritis and sever hip dysplasia have improved. Debbie and Homer are now taking walks twice a day. Debbie will foster him forever. No amount of money offered will get Homer away from his new home.

"Homer gave up hope – he was coming close to his end but he is happy now!" Debbie states. She has embraced imperfection and her eyes shine bright when she talks about Homer.

*****

Author's Note

The question is "why" did it take nine years and a brutally cold winter day for a neighbor to pick up the phone and call Animal Control? Although Homer's pen was attached to the back of this particular home, the home itself was located in an established neighborhood and in plain sight. This case of neglect and cruelty cannot be explained away with a location hidden in the countryside. Why did no one step up to save this helpless creature?

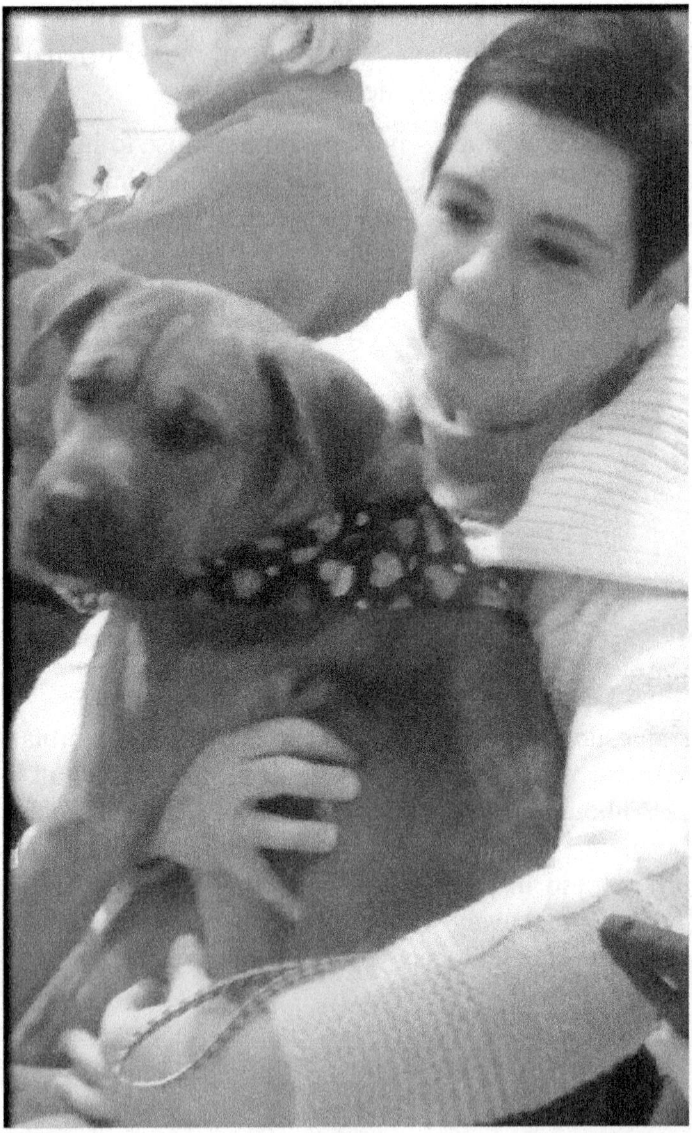

Ottis

Can't get it right Ottis

Brandy pulls into the parking lot of Pet Port, Vincennes City Shelter, silencing the engine of her Mini Cooper as she is taking a long deep and relaxing breath. It has been a tense day at the office and she could have stayed a couple more hours to work on her ever increasing stack of files.

Her neck and shoulders are tense and she is stretching to work out the kinks a bit while expecting her Mom to walk through the shelter door at any minute. It's a dreary November evening and it feels good just to sit a minute and relax in the silence of her car. All she can think of is to get a bite to eat and then go home to change into her comfy clothes. She is looking forward to be greeted by her kids, a beautiful Hungarian Sheepdog and an Old English Sheepdog. Brandy is planning for a quiet evening together with her Mom and the fur kids.

"Where is Mom?" Brandy is thinking while realizing that she has been waiting longer than usual. Brandy's Mom volunteers at the shelter but Brandy does not prefer to go inside. She usually waits outside in her car for Mom to finish up her volunteer work.

Controversy had been surrounding the shelter for some time. Rumors of unsanitary kennel conditions, improper housing of animals persisted along with concerns of animal abuse at the hands of the shelter employees. Allegations of euthanizing animals without valid reason made it hard for Brandy to step inside the shelter.

Just a few weeks ago the Mayor released the shelter director from her duties, along with her co-worker and boyfriend due to these horrendous conditions. An interim director, Ty Burks, was installed until a suitable replacement would be hired. *

Ready to get her evening started and having waited longer than usual, Brandy reluctantly entered the shelter to find out what is holding up her Mom. The building is filthy and the smell of urine and feces hangs heavily in the air making Brandy's eyes well up with tears. Hesitantly she went to the back part of the building in search for her Mom when she sees a small brown dog flopping and thrashing in his crate.

Crates stacked on top of each other line the walls and they are stacked three crates high. The young brown boxer mix is inside one of the top cages. His strange body movements of thrashing and flopping around remind her much of a fish of the water.

"What is wrong with him?" Brandy asks the director. "Well, this puppy came into the shelter with his Mom and her other puppies and we think he was fine when he arrived at the shelter. He may have been abused," Ty explains without going into too much detail at first. Brandy wants to know more about the puppy's history and keeps probing for more information.

In her conversation she finds out that a previous shelter worker was rumored to have used his fists hitting the animals in their heads or kicking them!

Although not a witness to the abuse, Ty shares this information he received by some of the remaining shelter staff upon taking over the duties as shelter director.

Brandy instinctively knows that this puppy may have been the recipient of some of those fisted blows. This small eight week young dog had been abused although there were no witnesses to the kind of abuse or his abuser.

"We believe someone left the crate open and the puppy fell out hitting the concrete floor" the director continues. Not only did this puppy fall out of his cage, his small body forcefully hitting the concrete floor, but an adult person is believed to have fallen on top of him too, crushing him with his body weight. As if this was not enough for a small puppy to endure, other unexplained abuse and pain may have been inflicted.

It is difficult to understand why this neglect and possible abuse was allowed to happen by the very same people whose job it was to take care of the animals entrusted to them while waiting for adoption into a new home.

"So what are you going to do with him?" Brandy asks. "We are going to put him down" Ty answers, meaning he will be euthanized. "He can't walk right; he is not adoptable."

Brandy was in disbelief of what all of her senses were telling her. She could feel a seldom experienced cold anger rise in her belly, directed at humans with no regard for the helpless animals they were supposed to care for.

At eight weeks young and fitting in the palm of her hand Brandy is outraged at the harsh treatment and pain this puppy most likely experienced. She just could not leave him behind in this filthy environment. "Well, can I have him?" she asks while outwardly keeping her composure and maintaining a cool exterior. "You can have him if you want him", Ty replies.

Glad that someone was interested in this puppy the director agrees for Brandy to take him to her veterinarian with the promise to bring him back later that evening. Brandy wanted to have this dog examined to make sure he was not in pain.

Veterinarian Dr. Mary Joe Collins, founder of the Lawrence County Animal Hospital, agrees to meet Brandy and the puppy on that same evening. After completion of a thorough examination and blood work a viral infection and toxins were ruled out. His reflexes were normal and his temperament was good.

However, the results of the blood work supported the possibility of trauma and a slow cerebral hemorrhage. The puppy displays symptoms of cerbellar ataxia , which means neurological trouble for this young dog.

"Symptoms of the disorder are located to the part of the brain dealing with placement of limbs; the inability of knowing his awareness in space. The puppy acted much like a person afflicted with the human disorder of cerebral palsy", explains Dr. Collins.

Dr. Collins prescribes anti-inflammatory medication to ease possible pain and inflammation likely to be sustained from the fall out of the cage, the weight from an adult human falling on him, or the possible blows he may have received to his head.

The damage to this tiny dog has most likely been caused by human hands and is irreversible. This puppy's brain is damaged, resulting of the loss of limb coordination and balance.

Dr. Collins explains the difficulties everyday life will bring for a dog with this disorder and the persons caring for him. Medication to help ease the symptoms will be expensive but more importantly the patience needed to care for such a dog would be exhausting. This puppy will grow into a medium size dog with special needs and it will take a special person to care for him. Would Brandy be that person?

Reluctantly Brandy is returning the puppy to the shelter as promised. Thinking about returning him makes her feel ill. She really does not want to let him go back but it will only be for one more night. Brandy agreed to return him and she would keep her promise. The adoption paperwork would be completed the next day and the puppy would leave the shelter with Brandy. She would rescue this little guy against all odds of him ever leading a normal doggie life.

As Brandy arrives at the shelter almost everyone is gone for the day and the main door is locked. She enters the building through the back door where she meets a shelter worker. The lights have been turned off and the building is mostly dark. The only light is coming from his office dimly illuminating the back hallway. Together they are going to the room in which the kennels are housed.

As the light comes on Brandy screams.

"The floor was literally moving! Cockroaches covered every square inch of the floor - their scattering creating the illusion of a rolling wave! When I looked into the cages I saw the animals covered with roaches and their food bowls overrun with them. It was disgusting and sickening and I absolutely would not leave the puppy there!" Brandy exclaimed.

Returning home Brandy was angry at what she experienced from the time she stepped into the shelter to pick up her Mom. Her plans for a quiet relaxing evening were shattered along with her trust in the safety of every animal housed at Pet Port, the shelter operated by the city.

Refusing to leave the puppy at the shelter he was rescued and safe at home with Brandy, protected from further harm.

The puppy was named Ottis. Of old German and English origin Ottis means "wealth. This is indeed an interesting choice of name. Interesting because Ottis has enriched the lives of everyone he is close to and helps caring for him. "He has brought so much joy into our lives and we love him so very much" Brandy explains.

Ottis is now 16 months old and just about fully grown. He has the features of a boxer with a shiny brown coat and large, dark trusting eyes. He is loved and cared for by Brandy, her Mom Jackie and Brandy's boyfriend Blaine.

Ottis is a traveling dog who lives with Brandy and Jackie in the city during the week and spends his weekends in the country together with Brandy and Blaine on Blaine's farm.

"He is a funny dog with a goofy personality" Brandy smiles. Throughout the week Jackie cares for him while Brandy works in the city. Brandy's other fur kids – tow large Sheepdogs- keep Ottis company. They have accepted him into their pack although Ottis can't keep up with them, much as he tries.

Life with Ottis is filled with challenges. These challenges will not go away but may intensify as Ottis grows older. Ottis' gait is very much off balance. His coordination and balance is severely affected by his condition. The rewards of life with Ottis are pure and simple joys watching him being happy and celebrating his successes.

While sauntering down the hallway Ottis appears to be drunk. His step is overextended; his legs are sliding out causing him to fall down often. Mostly he finds a way to get up again on his own and growls at anyone offering assistance. However, occasionally he falls onto his side and can't get up on his own. He knows he needs help and allows for being picked up.

"Ottis would love to be able to run. He tries so hard but he just can't" Brandy says. "The closest he comes to running is when he is super excited. All four of his legs lift off the floor at the same time – Ottis hops like a rabbit" she laughs.

Tremors and head shaking turn the simple task of eating into a big challenge. Ottis can't track well or focus well with his eyes. Erratic eye movements make it difficult for him to follow Brandy's hand moving in front of him. He can take treats from the hand holding it but only when the treat is directly held in front of him. When the hand moves he loses focus. His eyes roll and jump all over and he will miss grabbing the treat.

These tremors and head shaking make it impossible for Ottis to eat his food out of a dog bowl. Brandy explains that Ottis will take his food by lying on the floor with his food spread out in front of him.

"Although Ottis is carrying his head well enough, his head shakes back and forth unless he is sleeping. He jerks pretty badly when he sleeps" Brandy says. Severe muscle contractions shake his body while he is resting

Nonetheless, Ottis is visibly happy. He loves his family and his family loves him.

When Brandy is busy and away at work, Ottis stays in the care of her Mom Jackie and in the company of the two sheepdogs. In his city home Ottis enjoys spending time outside where a fenced yard keeps him and his playmates safe.

"He is fascinated with birds and loves to sit and watch them fly around. This makes him happy. He could sit there for hours and watch the birds but he tires fast. He plays hard for short periods of time and then crashes for quite a while" says Brandy.

During extreme weather conditions such as extreme cold or heat Ottis is only allowed outside for short periods of time. When exposed to these conditions for only a limited time his body shakes uncontrollably.

*****

TGIF – Friday afternoon has arrived and Brandy is ready to begin the long awaited weekend in the country with her boyfriend Blaine and Ottis.

Ottis' bag is packed and he too is ready to spend the weekend on the farm. When Blaine arrives to pick him up Ottis is excited to see Blaine and greets him happily, his body flopping and shaking from excitement of welcoming his long lost friend.

Just like every Friday evening Ottis is riding with Blaine in his truck ahead of Brandy. He is lying on his blanket on the back seat of the truck observing everything with his wandering eyes when they take off on their short drive to the farm. Brandy plans on running some errands before joining the crew for the weekend.

Just a short time later Brandy is on her way to the store when her phone rings and it is Blaine calling. Curious if he forgot something or needed her to pick up anything, she answers her phone.

"You won't believe what Ottis did!" he exclaims. Ottis who usually is on good behavior and fairly quiet when riding on the highway had an accident in the truck – an accident of the smelly kind. Ottis went to the bathroom in the truck!

As Blaine minds his own business and is paying attention to the flow of traffic a strong pungent odor is wafting to the front of the cabin. Quickly the smell turns into a horrendous stink. Ottis, unable to control his bowls, soiled the blanket he is lying on.

Blaine can't stand to remain in the smelly cabin with the stench locked tight in his nostrils. The open window does little to help. Unable to drive one more minute, Blaine pulls up to the side of the road to clean out the cabin as best as he can. After a rough cleaning he waves the blanket much like a bull fighter waves his cape. He tries to air out the blanket while directing traffic around him – a spectacle to be sure!

This is the first time Ottis has had an accident in the car. Usually he is pretty good but when he is excited he loses control of his bowels.

"Because of his condition it is very difficult for him to relieve himself like a normal dog would," Brandy says. Papers are laid out in certain areas of the house and Ottis knows they are his potty pads.

"He is not able to alert us and then wait for us to take him outside to do his business," Brandy continues.

To complicate things, a slippery surface will send Ottis sprawling, sending his legs straight out from under him. To ease his way, runners are leading the path to his potty pads to keep his falling to a minimum.

Unable to control his body from shaking and to maintain a steady stance he often steps right through the soiled pads. Much like a baby in diapers he needs cleaning of his paws after almost every potty break.

Blaine - who loves and helps caring for Ottis - knows he is not to blame for this mishap but is glad when they finally arrive at the farm on this evening.

*****

The farm is a fun place. Ottis is greeted by Momma, Sissy, Buster and Mable Ann– the resident farm dogs.

No one remembers for sure where Momma and Buster came from. One day they showed up at a neighboring farm, malnourished and wary of every human trying to come too close. With Momma being pregnant they made their home out in the pasture under an old discarded school bus. Sissy is the only remaining dog from Momma's litter.

Brandy and Blaine would take food and water to them and over the period of several months the dogs moved a little closer and made their new home under a large hay bale near the house.

Slowly all dogs gained confidence and trust in Brandy and Blaine and one day allowed for their reaching hands to make contact to receive their gentle touch. Since that day they have taken their place on the farm where they now belong to Blaine and Brandy. "Buster's ears were covered in ticks. I have never seen anything so bad in my life! We took them all to the Vet to be examined and to have the ticks removed from Buster's ears" Brandy explains.

Just a few months before Ottis' adoption, dog number four - Mable Ann- appeared on the farm. One day she was just there. Most likely she was no longer wanted by her owner and she was dropped off.

About nine months old at her arrival on the farm, Momma, Sissy and Buster hesitantly accepted her into their pack. "They are temperamental with her and don't always play nice. She has grown into large dog but is still somewhat of an outcast within the pack," Brandy says.

When Ottis joined the family a short time later, Mable Ann and Ottis became best friend. "This large goofy dog and Ottis formed a special bond. Mable is very tolerant and loves to play with Ottis. She doesn't quite understand why Ottis can't run and play with her…but Ottis loves Mable Ann" Brandy smiles.

The inseparable three have accepted Ottis into their pack as well. As much as Ottis wants to play with them he physically can't keep up. Their play is often rough and they love to run and play a game of chase; a game Ottis' conditions will not allow him to participate in. They simply knock him over not realizing he won't be able to join in.

One thing all the dogs love and can join in together is taking car rides in "their" car. A station wagon with the license plate reading "DGWGN" is the pleasure ride for these five fur kids. All are piling up in the back; Ottis with Brandy's or Blaine's help joins into the fun. On these rides they all band together and Ottis is truly a member of the pack. It is a sight to see, for they excitedly wag their tales, ready to go on their joy ride.

*****

Ottis typically is a sweet boy …unless one of his humans is leaving the home. At this precise moment he throws temper tantrums that easily compare to a two-year old toddler with a bad case of fits. He throws himself on the floor, thrashing and flailing all around while howling and screaming at the top of his lungs. It is impossible to ignore Ottis; especially for Brandy who will receive a special brand of tantrums when she is trying to leave. "He throws really bad fits. It's like he is almost hysterical. He tries to bite my arm but really can't. His bite is not strong at all. But…it's loving Ottis! It's like having a little child" Brandy says.

And just like a toddler, Ottis is easily distracted and pacified. A neat little trick, accidently discovered by Blaine, calms him down and restores his sweet temper. Blaine simply retreats into his bedroom, closes his door for a short time and allows Ottis to continue with his temper tantrum. After a short time, when the door opens and Blaine appears again Ottis is happy to see him and the woe of Brandy's leaving is forgotten.

The only other occasions when Ottis threw temper fits was when Brandy tried to leash him. Quickly Brandy learned that Ottis would fall and have difficulties to get up causing him to throw a king-size tantrum. Very quickly Brandy gave up on the idea of trying to leash Ottis.

Ottis is happiest when in the company of his human family. He is a sweet dog one can't help but fall in love with. His pleasures are simple. Just like watching the birds fly high in the sky makes him happy, the sounds of the ocean along with the cries of seagull's calms and soothes him. He falls asleep to his CD playing the sounds of the ocean.

*****

It is easy to see the love Brandy carries in her heart for this special dog. Her love for Ottis shines in her eyes and her voice gives away the pride she feels when telling about his odd gait, the simple pleasure he enjoys, and yes…the temper tantrums too.

"Unconditional love" is no longer a cliché but a reality for Brandy. It takes an enormous amount of time, love, patience and endurance to care for this dog. Brandy, along with Jackie's and Blaine's help, cares for Ottis and caters to his needs without a single complaint. Instead "Ottis has brought us lots of pleasure and joy!" is what you will hear her say.

*****

To watch see what this disorder looks like visit:

https://www.youtube.com/watch?v=L8pVBE0VY0o

Author's Note

If would be a great injustice not to mention that Vincennes Animal Shelter has undergone a major transformation since the installation of the new director, Laura Ariel, and her staff just a little over one year ago.

Gone are the days that dogs were housed outside with little shelter or kennels with double and triple occupancy and exposed to neglect and abuse. Unlike the past, now all kennels are cleaned and sanitized daily and the animals are removed from their kennels during the cleanings.

No longer are sick animals housed next to healthy ones. A quarantine room holding seventeen kennels has been established. This is where all new arrivals spend their first five days to be observed and evaluated for possible illness or disease.

A pole barn housing twenty-four kennels is a separate building providing a healthy, safe and warm environment for large and giant sized dogs.

During this first year of change eight hundred dogs have been admitted and sheltered. Over five hundred of them found a new home through adoption, one hundred and sixty animals were returned to their owners and thanks to the newly implemented foster-to-adopt program many more are temporarily living in the care of families.

A new computer system is capable of tracking important data such as the number of animals taken in during any given period of time, average length of stay, rate of adoption etc. which will help them make their case for receiving funds. Interim director Ty Burks has been credited with initiating much of it. As a municipality the shelter relies on allocated funds (tax payer money) and of course donations.

Much has been done in the span of one year but much more still remains to be done and the budget is tight. Fundraising activities help with needed improvements.

Recently Pet Smart Charities has partnered with the shelter; an organization to help homeless pets all over the country. The Rescue Wagon program is dedicated to transporting animals from overpopulated shelters to facilities with a lesser population to give the animals a chance at faster adoption.

Visit Vincennes Animal Shelter on Face Book to see all about the exciting changes and activities designed to make their animals comfortable during their stay while facilitating programs within their community designed to promote adoptions.

https://www.facebook.com/pages/Vincennes-Animal-Shelter/557844857623447

*http://www.suncommercial.com/news

Abby

Abby – A Reverse Rescue

Abby is a lucky girl!

Perhaps you don't agree and that is okay.

If you ask Abby and the people close to her, you will find everyone agrees that her life was saved by one of her many loves …a beautiful and playful Golden Retriever.

Abby, a sweet 10 year young girl loves all dogs. With her petite, slender appearance and beautiful long hair pulled back in a ponytail she is as comfortable in a room full of dogs as she is hanging out with her girlfriends. Lucky for Abby, her Aunt owns a Pet Provisions and Doggie Day Care business - a place Abby loves to visit at any available opportunity where she plays with her furry friends and helps out with chores.

Helping with chores consists mostly of playing with her buddies in the play yard, or taking the dogs from the play yard to their owners at pickup time as she did on this fateful day that changed and ultimately saved her life…

On this particular Saturday in October, the morning shapes up to be a beautiful fall day. It is sunny and warm with just a hint of crispness in the air - a perfect day for Abby to spend with her Aunt and help to out wherever she can. After all, Abby already knows that she wants to work with animals when she grows up - perhaps become a Veterinarian. The day is spent with hanging around the store and playing with her dogs in the play yard; her favorite activity. She is so good with the dogs and the dogs love Abby in return. They are having fun together.

By now it is time for the dogs to come in from the outside and spend some time indoors in their play rooms until it is time for their busy owners to pick up their kids. Just like our human children, some of our furry kids are eager to come in and push and shove to be the first ones, others hang back and have to be called several times, squeezing out just a few more minutes in the play yard. Abby, unafraid of taking care of a good natured but a little rowdy Golden Retriever male, is in the middle of a push and shove match.

Abby gets pushed just a little bit harder than what she is used to – nothing harmful but just enough to notice a difference. As closing time approaches and Harper and Cricket are being picked up she is excited to have her book "Rescued - A Tale of Two Dogs" autographed by the authors.

This is something she is looking forward to do this weekend - reading about Harper, one of her favorite big dogs she helps take care of. Abby did not know she would not have a chance to read during this weekend at all.

Soon after coming home she started to complain about abdominal pain. With pain severe enough Abby's Mom, a Registered Nurse, makes the decision to take Abby to the emergency room where tests reveal the unthinkable - a tumor on her kidney is detected.

*****

Four days later

Surgery is about to begin. In her big hospital bed, oversized hospital gown, with her parents by her side Abby is ready to fight the battle of her life. True to the character of this brave young girl she is giving comfort to her family by staring straight into the dark unknown, pushing all doubts aside – she is fighting and she is fighting to win. She is ready to be wheeled into the OR and ready for surgery to finally begin. She is ready to get this over with and deal with whatever comes her way. The author is amazed at this girl's strength, wisdom and tenacity – you see Abby was just told that she has a grapefruit size tumor on her kidney.....The prognosis was possible cancer which could result in the removal of her entire kidney.

Fear became reality – the tumor was cancerous and her kidney was removed. And so the struggles of a 10-year old girl with a heart of gold would begin. Recovering fairly quickly from the surgery itself, Abby felt all right. Over the next couple of weeks she was healing and working on regaining her strength. Strength, physically and emotionally, she would need to withstand the effects of chemotherapy that was soon to follow.

As Thanksgiving Day arrived Abby finds herself back at the Hospital. Sick from the harsh treatments of chemotherapy, she appears tiny and frail. Not only physically weakened, Abby's emotional state of mind is matching her physical appearance. She has become frail and withdrawn. With her family by her side "Thanksgiving" has a different meaning this year. Hearts are heavy at the sight of this pale, thin girl who just a few weeks ago was thriving, happy and seemingly healthy.

This year Thanksgiving Day would be spent loving and encouraging Abby to stay strong. Prayers are sent asking for the return of the former happy and healthy girl.

And those prayers will be answered. In the days to follow Abby is starting to feel better, she is able to eat a little more and once in a while a smile lightens up her still pale and tiny face.

It is Christmas now and Abby is home again!

Christmas, a joyful day celebrated in many homes across the country, is celebrated with a special prayer of thanks. Grateful for Abby's recovery but also thankful for sending one particular rowdy Golden Retriever who accidently pushed Abby just a bit too hard on that day in the play yard. Giving thanks to this accidental push from a favorite Golden Retriever for Abby to experience the pain and bleeding on that evening, followed by the rush to the Hospital. Lucky for Abby – perhaps without the bump from her furry friend she would not have felt anything at all for a long time.

Perhaps no accident at all? Everyone knows a dog's sense of smell is far superior to humans. Many articles and accounts have been written about dogs sniffing out cancer. Did Abby's furry friend have such a nose and gave her warning when bumping into her?

Even while undergoing harsh and sickening chemo treatments one thing has not changed…Abby has a loving and compassionate soul who is already working on helping other children in similar situations; and she loves her dogs! Just three months later she is back at her aunt's store fussing over her favorite dog who loves to receive her attention as much as she loves to lavish it on him. She almost is a typical 10-year old girl again, with a beautiful smile and a colorful hat with braids that resemble her once long tresses.

Leading her family and friends in the "Abby's dogs lick cancer" campaign she is raising funds to make a difference. She is collecting donations for the Children's Hospital where she underwent surgery to help other children in similar circumstances. A truly remarkable girl with a love for all dogs – and a girl who's life may have been saved by one of "her" dogs.

*****

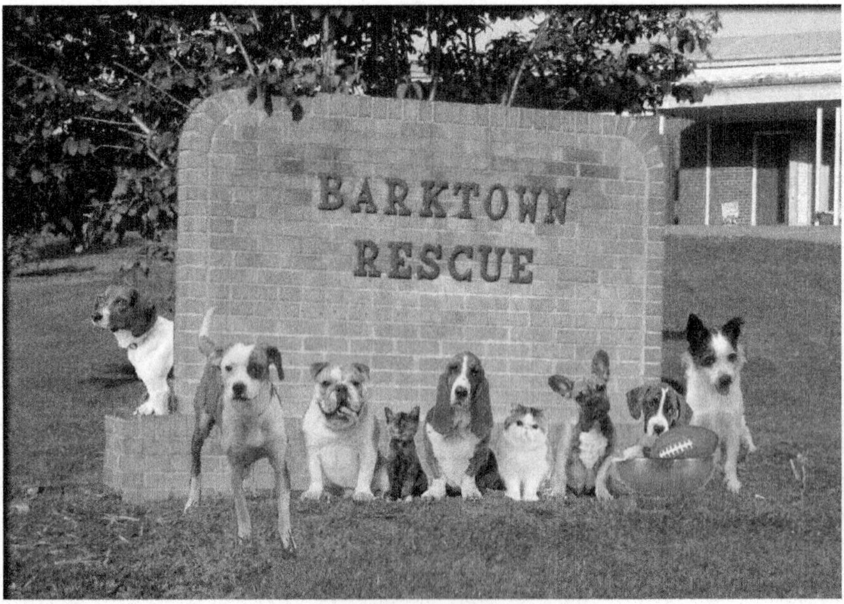

BarkTown Rescue

Barktown Rescue

Once upon a time there was a beautiful little girl with brown eyes and golden locks. She lived with her parents in a small rural Kentucky town. The little girl was no ordinary girl. She loved to play outside and explore her backyard and surrounding fields and meadows.

Especially animals – all animals, small and big - fascinated the little girl. She would delight in counting tadpoles hurriedly swimming in murky water, catch butterflies and fireflies, or watch the hustle and bustle of ants and other insects going about their chores. But….of all animals she loved dogs and cats the most.

She would follow any stray dog attempting to "save" him or try to sneak him food so he would not have to be hungry. Cats and kittens would be watched over and protected – making sure they had shelter and were safe from any harm. She would not mind muddying her pretty clothes to save any animal.

Much to the dismay of her parents, she often would return home with a stray dog or kitten in tow, insisting these animals would need her protection and would not survive without her help.

Time went by and the little girl turned into a beautiful young woman who chose to turn her love and affection towards young children; and so she became a passionate elementary school teacher who absolutely adored and loved her students.

But…saving animals was still a passion of the young woman. One day she decided to volunteer at her local Humane Society in her spare time, along with a close friend. True to her passion and sensitive nature it did not take long before she once again did not mind "muddying her clothes" and taking matter in her own hands. So many animals needed to be saved and she would do everything possible to save as many lives as she could. Meet Suzanne Robertson Bridwell – Co-founder and Director of Barktown Rescue.

Previous stories told about the misfortune of abused and mistreated animals inflicted by cruel human hands. It is equally important to tell the stories of rescue organizations such as Barktown. Without the love for animals, dedication and sacrifice made by countless volunteers across the country, these animals would not have a voice to speak for them.

The passion of these volunteers runs deep. They stand up and take on the fight to improve conditions for these helpless creatures. They push to improve outdated laws, fight for implementation of much needed new laws to provide better protection for our furry friends, and to ask for punishment of those who lack the moral fiber to treat "man's best friend" humanely.

They save and take care of the discarded and unwanted animals. Often these animals are produced by scrupulous backyard breeders who lack the knowledge and qualification of a certified and registered breeder. Puppy mills are designed to produce quantity over quality for the sake of a fast and easy profit.

People like Suzanne Robertson Bridwell have made personal sacrifices to make a difference. Barktown Rescue started – as so many rescues do – as an all-volunteer, foster home based organization.

*****

Fast forward five years.

Today I am meeting Suzanne along with board member Cindy Thomas at the Nelson County Animal Control facility. Cindy, a freelance photographer and marketing director for Barktown Rescue will photograph potential animals to be "pulled" and placed with Barktown Rescue.

It is an icy cold January morning with low hanging grey clouds threatening to burst open at any time to shower everyone not smart enough to stay inside with freezing rain. My mood matches the grey sky as the car follows the winding road to Animal Control – I don't know what to expect or what will await us.

Arriving at my destination I see two buildings side by side separated by a parking lot. Not sure where to go, I am glad to be greeted by Suzanne and Cindy.

The first and larger building is identified as Animal Control with an arrow pointing towards the right side of the building simply stating "receiving". I have arrived at the County Animal Shelter; a place I dread to visit! I dread to visit it because I know in my heart that it is almost certain not every animal housed inside will find its way to a loving family or rescue organization.

I know some animals will be walking from their kennels through the grey metal door to be delivered straight into doggie heaven. They will be destroyed and disposed of. But visit I must. I must see for myself how these animals are housed and how they ended up at this facility.

To understand I must meet the people who are charged with caring for these animals and who ultimately have to make the life and death decisions. I want to know about their daily work and get to know them, if only on the surface.

Steeling myself to walk into the "dog pound" I am surprised that we walk instead across the parking lot to the second building. As we approach, I notice for the first time the large sign identifying this building as the Nelson County Humane Society. Suzanne explains that the Nelson County Animal Shelter is home to both - the Nelson County Humane Society and Nelson County Animal Protection.

Following Suzanne and Cindy, we are entering a small but bright reception area where we are warmly greeted.

The building is old but well kept, with cheerful wall colors and bright posters intended for decoration while being informative at the same time. The atmosphere is warm and inviting. It is also obvious that both of my guides are well known and are regulars at this facility. Introductions are made and right away it is apparent that everyone is taking pride in the work they do and I am a welcome guest to take a look around.

Julie the adoption specialist is taking us on a guided tour. She explains that their facility takes in as many dogs as they can from Animal Control next door, provided space is available, and oversees the Adoption Program for the shelter. To place as many animals as possible they work with many rescue organizations such as Barktown Rescue and organizations from surrounding counties. Extensive networking is the key to their success.

Entering through a glass door we are greeted by a "Wiener Dog" happily playing with one of the volunteers. He is enjoying his time out of the kennel and the human attention and interaction he is receiving.

One more glass door separates us from the large room housing the kennels which are placed along the walls. Walking into the room the first thing one sees is the puppy pen. A litter of six beagle puppies is huddling together fussed over by another volunteer. How cute!

As we are visiting with every dog, all the animals are excited to see us. Everyone is jumping and barking for attention "Pick me, pick me!" One can't help but see the hope in dark liquid eyes begging for attention and hoping that today will be their day, and "this" visitor will be the one taking them home.

Slowly we stop at each kennel to visit with each dog and read each card identifying their breed, age, gender and special notes.

Before I realize it, our visit is over. As we re-enter the lobby we watch as a previously adopted beagle mix is being returned. Just one week ago he was adopted but now is being returned because the animal is too "wild" and can't be kept in the apartment.

"This is no isolated case" Julie explains. "Especially after the Christmas Holiday when children go back to school, and parents return to work, the cute puppy becomes a liability no one has time for anymore" she continues. Roughly 30% of animals are being returned – a staggering number considering potential adopters have passed the pre-approval process and landlord approval has been obtained.

Upon leaving the building I am relieved to know that none of the animals will be destroyed. Every boarder's safety is guaranteed and everyone has a chance to find their "forever" home.

*****

As we journey across the parking lot to our next destination, the Nelson County Animal Shelter and Animal Control Building, my apprehension returns.

We are greeted by Chuck, a smiling, soft spoken and gentle man. He is drying his hands as he welcomes us into the building. It is obvious that he was busy cleaning kennels but he graciously interrupted his work to give me an overview of the workings of his facility. Again, it is apparent that my two guides, Suzanne and Cindy, are regular visitors and welcome guests. We are standing in a small lobby separating office space to our right from the kennels to our left, with a small hall leading out a heavy grey metal back door straight ahead. On the right wall, opposite the entry to the kennels, stands a large waist high deep freezer. Instantly overcome by a dreadful feeling, I am afraid to ask what the contents of the freezer may reveal.

As if reading my mind Chuck directs my attention to a large dry erase board mounted on the right to the kennel entrance and begins to explain. Every kennel is listed and numbered on the board and included the name and breed of the current occupant. Some of the spaces list a name of a rescue organization, meaning this rescue has claimed this dog. After a required five-day waiting period, the rescue can pick up the "inmates" and they will be safe. I see "Barktown Rescue" in two spots. Great! These pooches will be safe too. There are also a couple of blank spaces and I feel a bit of relief. It simply means that Chuck still has room should there be any surrenders or stray dogs being picked up.

We enter the kennel area and the noise is instantly deafening. There are only twenty two kennels and not everyone is occupied but every occupant makes sure his voice is heard. Every "inmate" is begging to be freed. Suzanne is here today to pick two more dogs to be rescued; a tough decision I am not sure how she will make.

Suzanne explains that her decision is largely based on the type of dogs she already has available for adoption and on the temperament of the dogs. Currently she has a number of beagle mixes available for adoption so she will be looking for other breeds. Dogs displaying severe food aggression, or other aggressions, are also off limits for her. She will have to rescue those who have a definite chance of adoption.

It won't be long and Suzanne has identified two potential dogs to be rescued. One small lab mix is catching her attention. His identifying card reads "Surrendered by owner because too hyper".

Another small dog, a black terrier type "mop", is scared out of his mind, growling and trying to hide under his bed. He presents a pitiful sight. He too catches her attention. It is clear the poor dog is scared in this strange and unfamiliar place. Suzanne cautiously enters the kennel and kneels close to him speaking in a low and gentle voice to him assuring him "Everything is okay". She is offering him a treat which he carefully takes out of her hand. A good sign!

Cindy is taking pictures of our hopefuls. She will later post "before and after" pictures on Barktown's website. As a professional photographer she knows to capture them in "just the right way" to play on the emotions of potential adopters and to give the animals the best chance possible.

After visiting with all the dogs, Suzanne asks to bring out the little lab mix to test his temperament. He is a sweet boy, approximately one year old, and during the next 30 minutes standing in the lobby he exhibits no signs of being hyper. To the contrary – he is laying calmly next to Cindy not moving or disturbing anyone. No one can detect a sign of this dog being hyper. The questions bears, what was the real reason his owner surrendered him? Suzanne decides this one will get a new temporary home at Barktown Rescue. He will have to stay one more day until his five-day waiting period is up and then he can be released into her care.

The one going home with her on this day is the little black "mop". He is trying to hide and squeeze under his bed again when Suzanne takes him out of his kennel. He is growling and putting up a little fight when she picks him up but to everyone's surprise his tail begins to wag as soon as the door of the kennel closes behind him. Still a bit uncertain, he takes a treat and begins to relax a little. His five day period has expired and he is ready to go home with Suzanne today.

*****

As we are coming to the end of our visit at Nelson County Animal Control, I am glad to know that six dogs are going to Barktown Rescue and are safe. They are saved by Suzanne; additional dogs have been claimed by other rescues.

During my visit I could see that the kennels were clean and the animals safe and well cared for. But this freezer in the hallway was still bothering me. Did it really contain what I thought it did? I had to ask the question.

The sad answer was that yes, it contained the bodies of euthanized animals. Suzanne and Chuck explain that animals determined to be severely aggressive or ill would be euthanized. The most humane method was being used for this grim task. The animals will be sedated before the fatal injection is administered.

On now rare occasions, when the shelter is filled at capacity and no more room is available, a healthy animal will be euthanized. These are the dogs that have been at the shelter the longest and have inched their way up to the top of the list.

Although animals are still being euthanized, the number of animals being killed has been reduced by almost 50% since Chuck took over as kennel manager.

While Chuck is the one who has to complete this grim task he has the greatest compassion for all animals. This kind man who in his second occupation drives the school bus for disabled children is available for animals whenever he is needed. Often he stays until late evening or meets someone late at the facility when no one else can help. He spends his weekend caring for the animals and he will do everything possible to avoid euthanizing a healthy animal.

As we are departing the facility I feel overwhelmed by the existing need to place animals into homes and families who can provide the necessary patience, love and care these animals so very much deserve. I begin to feel the heavy burden of the many rescuers much like Chuck, Suzanne and Julie who have made it their mission to not only make a difference in the life of these animals but try to educate about the importance of spaying and neutering and the dangers of backyard breeding.

A short time later, I am pulling up to the building known as The Old Boston Elementary School. A newly erected stone marker identifies the building as "Barktown Rescue". With that simple sign the passion of a little girl who wanted to save every animal she could and who later became an elementary school teacher has come full circle. Suzanne is the "head mistress" a.k.a shelter director for Barktown Rescue. The old school has been turned into a rescue facility which has made her dream to save many more animals come true.

Her dream of actually having a facility to house animals has been made possible by a generous donor and animal lover; a real life story that almost sounds like a fairy tale imagined by a Hollywood screenwriter.

Bruce Flint, a Texas multi-millionaire, native of Boston, MA and animal advocate was intrigued by the old school. He was contemplating purchasing a facility to temporarily house animals in transit from kill shelters to rescue organizations in other parts of the country. He was intrigued by this school and especially by the town it was located in. "Boston"...although in Kentucky, it was perfect!

The World Wide Web was the tool that brought Bruce and Suzanne together. Although much contemplation, research and hard work had to be done first, it did not take long at all before the deal was made. It has been nine months now since Suzanne met Bruce for the first time at Planning and Zoning to obtain the shelter approval and six months since the doors officially opened and the first "guest" was welcomed to the "Barktown Bed & Breakfast". It was a match made online! Suzanne's life has changed forever. She loves her new occupation and has no regrets. She left her job as teacher and is now very busy running the shelter.

However, once a teacher, always a teacher. Suzanne is using her new position to educate and promote the importance of spaying and neutering. While this is not a "new" message and everyone should be aware of this by now, it is a message that is still very much in need to be shared. Suzanne is visiting her previous school regularly to meet students and introduce them to the responsibility of caring for an animal. She recruits and teaches new volunteers on how to properly care for the animals in her facility. She promotes animal welfare and is leading the fight against animal cruelty and dog fighting rings in her city and county.

*****

Entering the building the brightly painted walls welcome us and guide the eyes along the long hallway…such a long hallway but then again I remember I am entering an old school building.

The first door on the right side leads to the nerve center of the operation, the office – a big room with desks that seem small in comparison. A large old fashioned blackboard lists all animals in residence.

The door to the left leads into a much smaller "meet and greet" room. Cheery walls and comfortable seating will allow possible adopters to spend time with their chosen animals and allow them to get to know each other.

Assistant Director Heather Hefley and Kennel Manager Debbie Waters are greeting me and are happy to show me around. The atmosphere is filled with excitement because today they can share the good news. Two of Barktowns puppies have been selected to play in this year's Puppy Bowl XI, hosted by Animal Planet TV!! Barktown Rescue, the only organization in Kentucky invited to participate, is buzzing with possibilities. TV interviews with local stations are set up and local newspapers carry their story. Hopeful to gain new foster families and most importantly new donors, the attention is most welcome.

As we proceed down the hall I can see much is needed in terms of renovation. The need is overwhelming. The building is cold but the animals are comfortable and most importantly, they are safe. An old antiquated heating system needs replacement. Ceilings and floors need to be replaced. Every "classroom" houses kennels and every kennel is filled.

My guides are covered in fleece and coveralls, wearing scarves and boots to stay warm. This inconvenience does not matter; talking about the animals brightens their faces, eyes shining bright and big smiles lighting up their faces. Their voices are laced with pride as they tell me about each and every animal in their care.

However, many people are involved in helping with the organization's mission every day. Typically unseen and in the background they help with fundraising activities, marketing, accounting, photography and everything else needed to assist the shelter with its ultimate goal of adoptions while securing the financing necessary to keep the shelter in operation.

With no doubt the new building is a huge blessing; it also comes with challenges that need to be met daily. Volunteers willing to work at the shelter are desperately needed. For now a handful of Volunteers along with a very small paid staff is letting out the dogs for their potty break, cleaning their kennels and making sure their bowls are filled with food and water. They do this three times a day, every day of the week without complaint so that their "fur guests" are well taken care of.

All this is a small price to pay for the ability to do what Suzanne -and everyone by her side- loves to do.

However, Suzanne and her small staff are working every day to change this balance. Recruiting new volunteers and donors is at the top of their list.

The addition of dog grooming service and dog boarding has generated a small income stream. After only six months of operation the shelter has been successful in placing a total of 335 animals with new families for the year. Many more exciting projects are planned for the future of the shelter. Adding additional services will generate additional income and secure the place of Barktown Rescue in Nelson County, Kentucky and beyond.

*****

Debbie explains that every adoption is a happy but bittersweet occasion. When her charges go home with their new families, she is happy for them while tears stain her cheeks as she watches them leave. She, along with everyone working at the shelter, has formed an attachment to the animals. Each animal is loved and treated as one of their own during their stay at their shelter.

It is their dream that one day the kennels will be vacant, the bowls will remain empty, no noise is coming from the "classrooms", the long hallway will remain silent, no unexpected drop-offs will occur and everyone will go home knowing their work is done.

Until this day arrives, please consider adopting from a shelter! If you cannot adopt, please become a donor! Any amount is appreciated and much needed – no amount is too small. Too many fur kids are counting on you!

Please visit www.Barktown.org

Acknowledgments

Thank you to all my friends who have helped making this book possible. To those who have so willingly given their time to share their stories with me I am most grateful to. Without their patience and willingness to answer my many questions the stories of these fur kids would not have come to light.

My deepest gratitude goes to the following rescuers for sharing the stories of their animals: Jim and Becky Collings for Hannah Mae and Honey Bea, Rebecca Eaves – Founder of The Arrow Fund for Frodo, Kimberly Marie for Ellie Mae, Walter and Janice Oster for Rosie and Liberty, Debbie Howell for Homer, Diane Shoffner and April Race for Abby, Brandy Worland for Ottis, and Suzanne Robertson Bridwell and the entire staff along with many volunteers for Barktown Rescue.

A special thank you to my best friend and fellow author Debra Wagner for offering her expert assistance with proof reading and editing, and her red pen! Thank you for being my editor but most of all, my best friend! Thank you to author and friend Marcia Tomasiello for her continued support. You are very special! Thank you both for encouraging me to continue telling these stories when doubts clouded my vision.

Thank you to Mary Ann McCall Miller and Debbie Smith for bearing with me and patiently listening, reading and giving feedback before going to print. You're friendship is very special; a true gift!

Many thanks to Rebecca Eaves, Founder of The Arrow Fund, and Leslie Spetz, Board Member of The Arrow Fund, two amazing women who both took time out of their super busy schedules to meet with me and allow me an inside look into some of their gut wrenching work of saving the most severely abused animals.

Thank you to Suzanne Robertson Bridwell, Founder of Barktown Rescue, along with her staff and all volunteers …all are amazing people! Thanks for allowing me to spend an entire day at the shelter, allowing me to tag along to experience the behind the scene daily work of a rescue organization. It broke my heart when we went to the County Shelter and Suzanne explained the process of "pulling" dogs to be saved. Selecting certain animals over others is a gut wrenching process that shatters her heart a little more every time she has to make a life and death decision.

Last but not least – many, many thanks to Erin Pike, who so freely shared her legal expertise and gave me the added confidence to continue on my path.

You are all very special and I love you for who you are and what you do!

Previously Published -

"Rescued: A Tale of Two Dogs"

Tis' where the story begins.

Signed copies of both books are available at www.HarpersHouse.net

Order at a book store near you or online at
www.createspace.com/5006832
http://amazon.com/1505207533

Also available on Kindle
http://amazon.com/B00Q732RMS

Visit and like Harpers House on FB – join my mailing list for specials and upcoming projects

To contact author send email to:
 BirgitStubblefield@hotmail.com